Dances With Turtles

Dances With Turtles

YOU CAN'T MAKE THIS STUFF UP!

Russell Thornberry

ISBN: 1500321915
ISBN 13: 9781500321918
Library of Congress Control Number: 2015905377
CreateSpace Independent Publishing Platform
North Charleston, South Carolina

Table of Contents

Acknowledgements

THERE ARE MANY PEOPLE AND things that have contributed to the adventure/insanity and intrigue/torment that is my life! The adventure and intrigue trophy certainly goes to my wife, Sharleen, without whom I probably would have become a recluse living in a dark cave somewhere. She has made it possible for me to see the humor in life, which, as you read the following pages, you will realize is not always immediately apparent.

I am grateful to God for allowing me to survive some of the more traumatic events described in these pages. And I suppose I have him to thank for my weird sense of humor, by which I am urged to tell my often embarrassing stories for the sake of laughter.

I thank the squirrel, moose, deer, skunk, fish, etc., which have contributed to the many traumas that ended up funny in some strange way, and the doctors who have inspired me and, in some cases, saved my life.

Finally, I am grateful to my son, Darren, who is the best editor I could ask for. If you need a great editor, look him up at redpeneditingservice.com. He'll make you look downright intelligent.

CHAPTER 1

To Catch A Bass

Growing up on Texas' Gulf Coast, most of my fishing experience was in salt water. I had read plenty about bass fishing (Texas is one of the better bass fishing states), but I was 17 before I got my first crack at a bass. It was an off-the-wall opportunity at best, but when you're young, you don't always count the cost of your next adventure until it's already too expensive.

Drew Lawrence played banjo and I played guitar in a folk duo back in the mid 60s when folk music was all the rage. We sang and played at hometown events, mostly for the love of music. It certainly wasn't a lucrative endeavor. Then we got our big break ... a chance to perform at a University of Texas fraternity party in Austin. That was big stuff to us.

Being helpless, if not hopeless, fishing nuts, we planned to round out our trip to Austin with some bass fishing on our way home. I had heard of a lake near Uvalde where largemouth bass were supposedly plentiful. What could have been better than to combine our out-of-town musical debut with our first bass fishing trip? Yes, this was going to be THE life ... performing at night and fishing by day.

On the appointed Saturday night, we found our way to the frat party. It was in a big barn in the country, a few miles outside the Austin city limits. Drew had to park the Volkswagen Bug a quarter of a mile from the barn because of all the other cars. There must have been 500. There was going to be a real crowd. We were sure we were the reason. The word about our duo had gotten out.

Upon locating the fellow who had contracted us, we learned that we would be singing for 30 minutes beginning at midnight, and we'd be paid right after we finished. Seemed odd that we would be performing so late, but maybe that's how it was in the big time. Meanwhile we stood around and watched the party progress. And progress it did. Beer kegs lined the walls, and within an hour there wasn't a sober soul in the barn.

"Gonna be a long night," Drew groaned. "I didn't realize we'd been hired to sing for a beer bash."

"Ya wanna just leave?" I asked.

"Naw, we can't," he said. "We don't have enough gas money to get home 'til we get paid. Guess we'll have to hang around 'til then."

The night dragged on painfully. It was a sight to see ... all those folks staggering around, dancing and hanging on to each other with one hand and a beer in the other. It was not at all what we expected, but being a small town act with limited experience, we had no idea what we had gotten into. Our previous experiences with colleges were hootenannies, which were always pretty civilized. But this was a whole new ball game.

Drew and I climbed up to the hayloft to stay out of the way. As it neared midnight we were leaning on the rail overlooking the party below. "Man," Drew muttered, "I can hardly wait to sing for this crowd. They're so bombed they won't even know we're here."

Then a delirious frat boy arrived in the loft with a plastic cup full of beer. "How you guys doin'?" he slurred.

"Fine, thanks," we retorted in unison.

"Wouldja look at all those fools down there," the fellow mumbled as he leaned against the railing, gazing down at the couples dancing below. "Looky there at that one with the beehive on her head," he said pointing to a girl who was preoccupied with her dance partner. "Wonder what she'd do if I poured this beer right down that hole in the top of that beehive hairdo?"

"Hey pal," Drew offered, "you don't really want to do that ... do you?"

"Sure I do," he grinned. And with that he emptied his cup in the unsuspecting girl's mountain of hair.

What happened next was unbelievable.

Ms. Beehive jumped back from her dance partner in shock, thinking he was the culprit. With a heated remark, she raised her cup of beer and dashed it into his face. The poor fellow had no idea what provoked her, but he wasn't going to take a face full of beer sitting down. His cup was still full so he splashed it into her face, and the war was on. Suddenly everybody was splashing beer into everyone else's faces. Within seconds party patrons were running to the beer kegs along the walls, filling their glasses, and running back to the center of the dance floor to douse each other again. Then back to the beer kegs they'd go and repeat the whole performance. It was obvious that this event was to be the highlight of the party. The fellow who started it all was in hysterics.

At this point it was obvious that our performance was in jeopardy. I suggested to Drew that we vacate the premises before the party turned into a full-scale riot. He agreed so we grabbed our guitar and banjo and headed for the car.

Since we left without being paid, much less performing, our lack of funds posed a problem. The plan had been to go as far as Uvalde that night. Drew figured we had about enough gas to get there. He suggested we go that far and then figure out our next move. I had no better idea, so we headed south in the middle of the night.

En route to Uvalde the bottom fell out of the black Texas sky, and it rained so hard the windshield wipers couldn't handle it. Several times we had to pull over because we couldn't see the highway. We were getting weary. We'd been on our feet for 20 hours when we pulled into Uvalde at 2 a.m. It was still raining cats and dogs, which eliminated our former option of sleeping out under the stars. We were out of money, and according to the gas gauge, the Bug was running on fumes.

We just wanted to sleep. That wasn't possible in a Bug, however, so we pulled over at the edge of town to develop a plan.

"Ya know anybody in Uvalde?" Drew yawned.

"Not a soul," I said.

"Gotta be someplace where we can sleep in this town," he grumbled, stretching and rubbing his eyes. Then he sat up at full alert and said, "Hey, maybe we could stay in jail overnight!"

"Jail?" I shrugged. "How we gonna do that?" "There's gotta be a way," he mused.

"How do you get in jail without committing a crime?" I asked.

"I dunno," he said, "but there's gotta be a way. Maybe we'll have to commit a crime to get in?"

"Oh, great," I said in total disgust. "First, some beer-soaked ding-a-ling wrecks our musical career, and now we're gonna have to commit some stupid crime just so we can get a good night's sleep. This is nuts."

Totally oblivious to my ranting, Drew announced that we'd just have to figure out what crime would net a sentence of one night in jail.

For a moment the only sound was that of heavy rain rattling against the forlorn little car. Then Drew asked, "Can you get thrown in jail for runnin' a stop sign?"

"I don't think so," I replied. "I think you can get a ticket, but probably not thrown in jail. Why don't we just go ask somebody at the police station if they could put us up for the night? The worst thing they could say is no."

We drove around until we located the sheriff's office, but we lost our nerve when it came to asking for a cell for the night. "I think I'll just drive around the block on the wrong side of the street," Drew announced. "Then if we get stopped, we can pop the question."

It was a hair-brained scheme, but the best we had. Unfortunately, at 2 a.m. in Uvalde, Texas, there's no one around to notice which side of the street you drive on. Drew drove round and round the block to no avail. Finally the hopelessness took a humorous turn. We knew that at any moment our last ditch effort would disintegrate. The fumes couldn't last much longer.

"Can you believe this?" Drew howled. "If I didn't want to get caught right now, there'd be cops on every corner. But here I am, trying my best to get stopped, and I can't get arrested."

It was pretty funny. Soon we were both laughing so hard that tears were streaming from our eyes. Every time we passed by the sheriff's office again, on the wrong side of the road, we laughed even harder.

"Ain't we a picture of success?" Drew shrieked. "Yessir, we're big time stars now. I'm sure this is how all the stars do it."

I was laughing too hard to talk when I happened to look through tear-filled eyes into the rearview mirror. There, a block behind us, was a flashing red light. "Drew," I gasped, "at last, we've been rescued. Here comes the man in blue!"

Drew pulled over in anticipation. We wiped our eyes on our sleeves and tried to compose ourselves. After all, we wanted to keep our offense to a bare minimum. If the officer saw us in hysterics, he might suspect we weren't playing with a full deck.

The car pulled up behind us and out stepped a young constable who didn't appear to be much older than us. He walked cautiously up to Drew's door and shined his flashlight into his face, and then into mine. In his most official voice, he asked, "You boys lookin' to gitcherselfs th'owed in jail?"

His question was simply too much to bear. We exploded into fits of uncontrollable laughter. We could hardly breathe, much less answer the question. The officer was obviously bewildered. He just stood there with a puzzled look on his face while Drew and I nearly lost it all. Fighting for control, Drew finally gasped in reply, "That's kinda what we had in mind!"

Eventually the young officer suggested that we get ourselves under control, and somehow we did. We explained that we were in need of a room (or a cell, as it were) for the night, and asked the officer if he could assist us.

The truth was, he explained, he didn't have the authority to put us in jail. The only way it could be arranged was for him to call the sheriff and ask him to do it. We were in total agreement, so he took us inside the station.

Twenty minutes later the sheriff walked in and all the joviality evaporated. He was not amused by this intrusion on his sleep. He walked past us, sat down behind his desk, propped his feet on the desk, folded his hands behind his head and looked at us with a stare that would have burned holes through concrete. "Whatter you young punks doin' here?" he growled.

Begging his official pardon, we explained our plight and asked for his mercy in this most humiliating situation.

He closed his eyes and sat quietly for a long while, as if contemplating our sentence. Drew and I squirmed. What once seemed like the innocent pursuit of a place to sleep now appeared to take on the atmosphere of "death row."

I looked at Drew out of the corner of my eye. I'm certain that I saw him trembling under the pressure of the impending verdict. I felt a sick empty feeling in the pit of my stomach.

After an eternity of deathly silence, the sheriff opened his eyes. He looked down at our instrument cases and asked us what they were. We explained that one was a banjo and the other was a guitar. "Can ya play 'em?" he asked flatly.

"Yessir," we chirped.

"Are ya any good?"

"Uh, well, we think we're fair," Drew said, almost apologetically.

The sheriff rubbed his eyes for a moment and said, "Okay boys ... play me somethin'. If I like it, I'll lock you up."

Wow ... what an opportunity! I swallowed hard. This was going to be the performance of our lives. If the sheriff liked us we'd get put in jail. I didn't want to know where we'd end up if he didn't like us. So there, in front of the sheriff's desk, at 3 a.m., Drew and I played and sang our hearts out under a kind of pressure that we'd never experienced in our young lives in show biz.

When we finished our song, the sheriff told us to keep on playing. And play we did. Thirty minutes later we were still playing our hearts out. All the while the sheriff just sat there with his eyes closed, hands behind his head, feet on his desk. As we finished a rounding chorus of "Old Stewball Was A Racehorse," the sheriff opened his eyes and said, "Y'all ain't too bad. I reckon I can letcha stay the night."

Drew and I sighed in relief.

"Only thing is," he drawled, "Can't putcha in an open cell. Law says the cell's gotta be locked if somebody's in it."

He showed us to a cell with two bunks. We walked in and he closed the metal door and locked it. I remember the incredible sinking feeling as it clanged shut. Never had I sung and played with such conviction (pun intended) ... And now, this strange reward.

"Any pa'tickler time you boys want out?" the sheriff asked as he walked away.

"Yessir ... 'bout 8:00 would be fine." I said. "We were sorta planning to do a little bass fishin' in the mornin' ... right after we wire home for more money. That is, if the rain lets up."

CHAPTER 2

Fishing Stinks

IN THE 70S, GUIDING FLY fishermen on the lower Bow River between Calgary and Carseland, Alberta, was a fairly simple job. It generally meant keeping the drift boat a short cast from the bank. The spectacular river usually took care of the rest by producing large, voracious trout in amazing numbers.

On a good day, anyone possessing enough motor skills to row a boat could pass for a fishing guide. On a bad day, Izaak Walton might have been reduced to a blithering ninny, rowing through a great troutless void.

Two things tormented the fishing guides on the famous Bow. The first was rising water. The reservoir above Calgary seemed to be manned by a devout anti-fisherman who opened the gates of the dam and let water through during prime daylight fishing hours. He could have done this by night, but no one would be fishing ... so why bother? Somehow he found out that the fish are most uncooperative when the river is on the rise, so when the reservoir had plenty of water, he delighted in opening his floodgates and ruining the fishing. Sure, I know that southern Alberta needed the water for irrigation, but water was made for fishing. Right?

The second problem was, and still is, the wind, which can blow 2,000 miles an hour in the river valley. It's not unlike the Boeing Wind Tunnel. It makes turning over a light leader like throwing feathers into a gale. Casting a weighted Woolly Bugger into such a wind will cripple even the strongest caster in short order.

Then there were those choice days when the Mad Gate Opener teamed up with the Keeper of The Wind, and jointly they cursed the river valley with rising water and hurricane-force winds. Those days put river guides to the supreme test. In those instances, I had the urge to jump from a high bank and impale myself on the sharp end of my expensive ash oars. Only the fear of somehow surviving the attempt kept me from trying it!

It was on such a windy day that I was rowing with wretched desperation, trying to make the stubborn Mackenzie boat go with the current while the wind held me in place. It's depressing when the wind overrules the laws of nature. The whole object of drifting a river is the delight of the quiet ride with the current. I hated to pay such a price for what Mother Nature promised for free. My fishermen were determined but beaten by the wind. The rising water put the fish off their feed and we couldn't get arrested with a streamer. Occasionally, I would spot a fish rising cautiously, being ever so careful not to open its mouth too wide for fear of catching the wind and being blown up like a weather balloon.

One of my anglers, casting into the wind to a rising trout, buried his Royal Humpy in his cheek on a crosswind back cast. The wind was blowing so violently that the leader blew off course, wrapped around his head, and snapped the fly off in his cheek! The poor fellow was too squeamish to let me pull it out, so it stayed there all day. In addition to the discomfort of being impaled on a size 12 trout hook, the winds kept catching the wings of the fly, causing it to flutter violently against his cheek, which resulted in a flinching, twitching of his right eye not unlike the tormented twitch on the face of Inspector Jacques Clouseau's superior officer after being humiliated by one of his maddening stunts.

Fish were not to be had under the circumstances, so we agreed to pull up on a steep bank and wait for dusk and hopefully lower water and a diminishing wind. In the meantime, my two defeated clients bedded down on the grass on the downwind side of the boat and took a nap.

After a couple of hours the wind began to subside. I felt the need to inspire my clients, so I rigged up my streamer rod, tied on a magnum Woolly Bugger and quietly sneaked off the bank, careful not to awaken the two sleeping souls. If I could produce a fish, it might provide the necessary incentive for them to try again.

But the fish would not cooperate. A thousand casts and a quarter mile downstream, I hadn't turned a single one. There was a small eddy where the current curled around a rock formation and spun off the bank in a very fishy manner. I knew there had to be a fish there.

Casting from the only available position meant that I had to make my back cast almost straight up in order to avoid hanging up in the Timothy-grass growing on the hill behind me. The physical laws that govern fly casting state plainly that a vertical back cast will be followed by a weak and lifeless forward cast. The law held true and I floundered and dodged the ungainly streamer. I could almost reach the eddy ... another two feet and I could at least say I had tested it. Stripping a questionable length of line off my reel, I made a violent vertical back cast and then drove the rod tip forward, hoping to gain the necessary inches.

There's another law that says the closer you come to hitting your target, the greater the odds of hanging up your back cast. You may false cast 400 times without a hitch, but as you attempt to deliver the final forward cast, you hang up on something ... and I did.

The fly hung in the tall grass somewhere on the hill behind me. I tugged gently at first, but the fly would not come free. In frustration, I began really thrashing the rod, not wanting to have to climb out of the river to get free. The problem was above and behind me, and in desperation I gave a final sharp tug over my shoulder and turned to see what was wrong.

Oh, I saw clearly what was wrong: an extremely upset skunk wearing a size 2 weighted Woolly Bugger squarely in the end of his nose. He was rolling down the bank in a blur of black and white, heading right for me. He made a final bounce from the bank directly above my head, and I lunged upstream as the poor critter splashed down right where I'd been standing.

The swift current immediately swept the skunk downstream, screaming line off my reel, causing me to engage him as if he were a big fish. It was something of an out-of-body experience to be standing on the banks of Alberta's most famous trout stream fighting an aquatic skunk on a 6-weight trout rod. I remember thinking how well he fought, followed by a strange sense that I might actually be on Candid Camera.

After 10 minutes of battling, the current overwhelmed him and he became dead weight on the end of my line. Eventually I grabbed the line just ahead of the short, stout leader and lifted the soggy critter out of the water.

Most skunks meet their maker out on the highways at night. An 18-wheeler would have been downright pleasant compared with this. I felt sorry for the little fellow. What must the odds have been against us meeting like that? I felt helplessly guilty at first, but soon shifted the guilt to its rightful heir, the madman at the dam. If he hadn't opened the dam, the water would have been lower, the fish would have been cooperating, and I never would have been fishing anywhere near the skunk!

Next came the question of how to dispose of the poor creature.

I had no choice but to carry him back to the boat, where I could clip the 20-pound test leader. My fishermen were still lying in the grass, hiding from the wind, when I arrived.

"Any luck?" one asked nonchalantly, without even looking up.

I hesitated, searching for words. "Let's just say I got skunked," I replied.

The guy with the Royal Humpy stuck in his cheek said, in all innocence, "Yeah, some days fishin' stinks. Ha ha."

He glanced up and saw the skunk dangling from my fly line. His jaw dropped in disbelief as he stammered, “What the ...?”

“Good skunk rod,” I said. “Good stiff tip. Perfect when you tie into a real stinker in a strong current. Anybody got a pair of clippers?”

CHAPTER 3

Burgled

THE PHONE RANG AT 3:30 a.m. on a frozen January night in Edmonton, Alberta, in 1976. A police officer announced himself and asked if I was Russell Thornberry, the owner of The Fishin' Hole. I admitted that I was. Sadly, someone had broken into my little fly-fishing specialty shop. The officer suggested that I meet him at the store right away. I dressed quickly and drove across town through snowy streets. When I arrived, two officers were inside my store, already dusting the cash register for fingerprints.

"Looks like he was just after money," said the man in charge.

I was relieved. If the thief had decided to vandalize the store, it could have been disastrous. Fortunately there was only a little change in the register, and that's all he took.

I sat quietly as the officers continued to dust for fingerprints. A few minutes later, another patrol car pulled into the vacant parking lot. I unlocked the front door and admitted two more officers. One was a no-nonsense veteran. He went right to work. The second officer was a rosy-cheeked young man, probably not even 21. He had that shiny and new appearance, and it was obvious that he was quite impressed with the fact that he was a police officer. He strolled casually around my little shop, looking at the fish on the walls and the tackle hanging everywhere. "Oh, a fishing shop," he mused. "I do a little fishing."

"Oh great," I muttered to myself. "I'm gonna hear some fishing stories at four in the morning."

"Yeah," he continued, now gaining volume and conviction, "I bought that book 'Fishing Jasper National Park,' by that guy … uh … Russell Thornberry."

He had no clue who I was, but now he had my attention.

He continued, almost indignantly, rocking back on his heels with his hands clasped behind his back, "If I ever meet that S.O.B., I'm gonna tell him he's full of shit!"

The other officers rolled their eyes in disbelief. I could hardly believe my ears. Suddenly the entertainment value of the moment outweighed the inconvenience of the hour and circumstance. "Well, just let it all out," I encouraged.

"If I ever meet him, I will!" he scoffed.

"Well partner, you just did. I'm Russell Thornberry, and what's your name?"

I extended my hand.

The young cop instantly choked with embarrassment, sputtering and stumbling for words. It was all I could do not to break out in laughter, but somehow I managed to remain stone-faced.

"Hold the apology," I said. "Since time began, ten percent of the fishermen have caught ninety percent of the fish. If you don't fall into that ten percent, you certainly don't have to apologize to me!"

The poor guy made a pitiful sight. It was one of the greatest social blunders I had ever witnessed. Never have I seen a man with his mouth so full of his own two feet. It was a truly hysterical sight.

His superior apologized for him and they left. Finally I was alone, relieved that the break-in had been of so little consequence and truly tickled at the young officer's flat-footed faux pas.

But it wasn't the last I'd see of that young policeman. A few days later he came into my store during normal business hours, in full uniform. He had a buddy in plain clothes with him. The officer kept trying to get my attention so that he could point out the customer he had brought with him. That happened several times during the next few weeks, and each time it was the same. He went out of his way to point out another customer he had brought to my store. And each time it was a different customer. I often wondered if he was nabbing people for jaywalking and giving them the choice of a ticket or a trip to The Fishin' Hole to buy some tackle from me.

CHAPTER 4

Minipi Moike

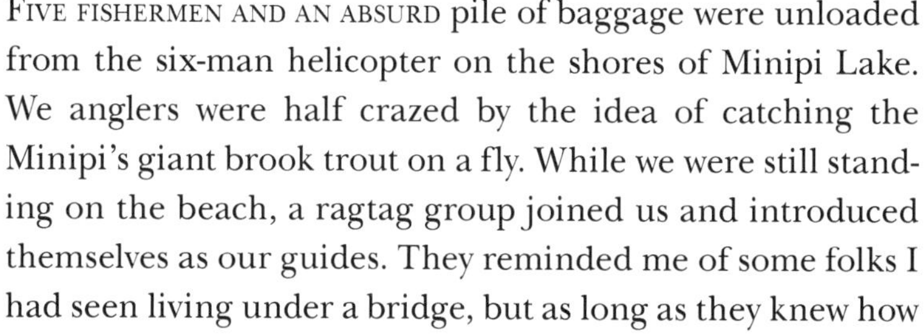

Five fishermen and an absurd pile of baggage were unloaded from the six-man helicopter on the shores of Minipi Lake. We anglers were half crazed by the idea of catching the Minipi's giant brook trout on a fly. While we were still standing on the beach, a ragtag group joined us and introduced themselves as our guides. They reminded me of some folks I had seen living under a bridge, but as long as they knew how to put us into big brookies, dress code and hygiene weren't important.

One of the incoming fishermen lit on his guide like a chicken on a June bug, in a fit of brook trout fever. To say he was excited would be a gross understatement. I still vividly remember his question:

Fisherman: "Well, what fly do you recommend?"

Guide: "Aw, just use whatcha usually uses."

Fisherman: "Golly, well, I've never fished for big brookies before. Could you be a little more specific?"

Guide: "Ah hell, I don't care, I hates fishin'!"

That set the tone. For these guides, it was not a labor of love. They were commercial fishermen, left without work thanks to Great Britain's ban on Canadian seafood. The ban on seal hunting had increased the population, which in turned reduced their catches. Greenpeace was all too happy to see the old salts starve. Though they didn't fit the picture of the "ideal" fishing guides, I felt sorry for them and was committed to make the most of it.

A young kid, maybe 18, walked up and introduced himself as Moike.

"Moike – now that's a very unusual name," I said.

"Moike's a usual name round these parts," he exclaimed.

"How is it spelled?" I inquired.

"M-I-K-E – Moike," he exclaimed, now indignant.

"Oh I get it," I said apologetically, "your name is Moike."

"Yeah, Moike," he grinned, "Ma name's Moike and I hates poike."

So, I'd determined that his name was Mike and that he hated pike – a toothy, torpedo-shaped fish that inhabits most Canadian waterways from British Columbia to Newfoundland.

This was my first encounter with Newfies (Newfoundlanders), who speak their own distinct version of English.

The following morning, my fishing partner Gary and I met Moike at the boat. We were decked out in the latest in quintessential fly-fishing duds and looked like we had stepped out of an Orvis catalog. Conversely, Moike was wearing jeans, running shoes and a heavy drab green fatigue coat, which appeared to have been issued by some ancient branch of the armed forces. The coat, while at least two sizes too large for Moike, was stuffed full of something in every pocket. He looked like an army green Pillsbury Doughboy, which begged the obvious questions ...

"Whatcha got in all those pockets?" Gary chirped.

"Rocks," Moike said flatly.

"Rocks?!" Gary echoed back with justifiable alarm. "Why would anybody get in a boat wearing a coat loaded with rocks?"

"I hates poike," Moike answered with that sinister grin. We were not in the company of a rank-and-file fly-fishing guide.

Gary's nervous eyes met mine, communicating unspoken concern.

All I could think of was how fast he would plummet to the icy bottom of Minipi Lake if he tipped a little too far and fell out of the boat. Moike showed no such concern. While I wanted to credit him with unusual bravery, I finally settled on unusual stupidity. That made more sense.

Gary and I caught some awesome brook trout that morning, some in the 6-pound range, which for brook trout is staggering. Consider that a 6-inch brookie in its native range of the Northeastern United States is considered front page new these days. They used to grow bigger there, but loss of natural habitat, water pollution and the stocking of non-native trout species have driven them to miniscule proportions. Thus the magic of the Minipi watershed.

A phenomenon occurred each night on Minipi Lake, and to this day I have no idea why. Fat mice or voles crawled into the cold water after dark and swam until hypothermia killed them. At dawn the lake was littered with the floating, furry little rodents. Stomach contents analysis showed that both the northern pike and the brook trout ate them like candy until their stomachs bulged. What resulted during the daylight hours were a lot of very satisfied fish.

I had used spun deer hair mouse flies in the South when fishing for largemouth bass and found them very effective when dropped on the water, twitching along in a slow swimming motion. Fortunately I had some in my large fly box, so I decided to try them on the mouse-eating fish of the Minipi.

I cast my mouse alongside a mat of floating grass, twitched it a couple of times, and the water erupted with a green explosion in the form of a huge northern pike. That brought Moike out of his seat. He was paying attention now. That was strangely comforting because until then Moike seemed to have engaged only a minimal number of brain cells in the task at hand.

The fight lasted about 15 minutes. Finally the big pike slid alongside the boat. Moike gulped him up into a dip net big enough for a dolphin. The obligatory high-fives, hollering and backslapping ensued as Moike lifted the long fish into the air with a scale hooked in his lip. In an instant a hush fell over the boat as we watched the scale bottom out at 20 pounds, indicating that this fish weighed something in excess of that.

At that instant Moike took over with the kind of mastery formerly credited only to sea captains under siege. He slammed the boat into forward and ran it right up onto dry ground, pitched the fish to the beach, brandished a previously unseen ax and chopped the pike in half. Then Moike weighed both ends and gleefully announced it was a 22-pounder.

The hush fell once more as Gary and I made the necessary mental adjustments.

Moike was simply elated. We were simply astonished.

"What if I wanted to have that fish mounted?" I asked Moike politely, since he was still holding his axe.

"I hates poike," he said, pushing the boat back in the water.

It was then that I realized that Moike might be two tacos short of a blue plate special – and an ax murderer to boot! Neither Gary nor I turned our backs on him for the remainder of the trip.

We continued to catch those big and beautiful brook trout, but even with our best effort to abstain, we occasionally caught pike. And when we did, Moike would grab the fish behind the head and pull rocks from any one of his many pockets and stuff them down the pike's throat until it could hold no more. Then he would drop it headfirst back into the water and cheer with delight as it sunk like a cannonball. It was a demented catch and release system. Judging by the number of rocks in his pockets, Moike was expecting us to catch lots of poike.

His finest moments, at least in his mind, were when he would grab a pike behind the head, slam the motor into reverse and jam the pike's long pointed snout into the spinning props, which sheared its kisser all the way to its eyes. Then Moike would hold up his prize and cackle, "I makes blunts of 'em!"

Moike looked for any way to amuse himself as he wiled away the days in boats with fly fishermen who spent more on a fly vest than he earned for two weeks of guiding. It was an odd and somewhat unnerving experience, but the big brook trout and a good fishing partner saved the week.

One bright afternoon, as we were passing through a narrows between two lakes, we saw a gigantic pike. We guessed it would crowd 50 pounds ... five feet long ... with the girth of a power pole. The sight of the great fish sent chills up my spine. Moike was gasping and drooling out both sides of his mouth, undoubtedly fantasizing about getting his ax into it. We watched the fish drift into deep water, vanishing like a ghost.

We talked at length about how we might entice the monster. Then there was the problem of handling it if we got it hooked. Gary and I found a huge treble hook the size of a man's open hand in the cook tent. With that, a plan was hatched. (Perhaps we had more in common with Moike than we thought.) We gathered up about 60 yards of parachute cord for the main line, three feet of soft wire for a leader and an empty bleach bottle for a bobber.

The next morning we slipped quietly into the narrows and spotted the big pike. We instructed Moike to go around it, pull the boat in 40 yards above it and drop anchor. There was a slight current flowing through the narrows. We were depending on it to tow our bait toward the giant pike. It shames me to admit that we used a 3-pound brook trout as live bait with the huge treble hook through its dorsal fin. It was suspended about four feet from the surface by the empty bleach jug bobber.

We held our breath as the bobber drifted to the target zone. When we were satisfied that it had arrived, we tied off the parachute cord to the boat and waited. That the pike of the Minipi dined regularly on brook trout was a given. No red blooded, 50-pound pike could resist a live brookie that couldn't get away.

The boat eventually drifted too far to the left and pulled the bobber out of the strike zone. We asked Moike to back the boat down a few yards and correct it in the current. As he did he caught the parachute in the prop. Before we could react, the motor was gobbling up the line and tearing our pike rigging to shreds. So ended our attempt to catch the world's most awesome northern pike.

Gary and I were bummed out, but Moike was crushed. We could tell that he had special plans for that fish. In retrospect I'm glad we didn't catch it. I'm not sure I could have endured watching Moike chop it into chunks.

After several days of fishing the little chain of moving lakes, Moike took us to the headwaters of the Minipi River. The water pinched in sharply from the lake and bulged as it fell off into the thundering falls. Mist hung in the air as the churning white water spilled down the terraced falls, which formed deep pools, one below the other, until the river finally flattened out at the bottom.

I grabbed my 6-weight fly rod with a floating line and a #6 white Muddler Minnow dangling from the end of a 6-pound tippet. As soon as the fly hit the white foam, it disappeared. I made one strip and felt the weight of a charging brook trout. Finally I lifted the 1½-pounder from the water and released it. In that top pool I caught similar sized brook trout as fast as I could get my fly back into the water.

I remembered reading about Lee Wulff, who is credited with discovering this fly-fishing bonanza, describing his first visit to the Minipi. He mentioned catching three brook trout at one time. That was an amazing feat, and in these waters it was very plausible. So, I tied on a tandem leader and another white Muddler Minnow. As soon as the flies touched down, I made an initial strip, and as before I felt the strike. I was playing that fish when I felt a bump and the added weight of a second trout. Eventually I brought them to hand – my first ever double while fly fishing for trout of any kind.

Quickly I tied on the second tandem leader and added a third fly. I cast the trio onto the thundering foam. Trout one hit immediately, and I distinctly remember the second trout adding his weight to the line, but they were fighting with such frenzy that I had no idea if I had actually hooked three. When I worked the trout to the edge of the pool, I could see only two, so I stripped off some slack line and let them dash around the pool again, essentially trolling the available fly as they went.

In seconds my rod bowed up like a Hula Hoop, and I knew I was in business. All three fish came splashing to hand, and I released them with gratitude. With that I reeled up my line and retired for the day. To make another cast would have been gluttonous.

On my second trip to the Minipi, I was introduced to my new guide, whose name was Dern. I assumed he was a Newfie, so I approached discussion about his name with caution.

"Dern," I said, "now that's an interesting name."

Dern did not respond.

Wanting to establish some form of communication, I pushed the issue.

"Tell me Dern, how do you spell Dern?"

"D-A-R-R-E-N – Dern," he answered.

"Oh, Dern!" I said. "You're not going to believe this, but I have a son named Dern."

"Ah," said Dern, and that was that.

It's not that I want a blabbermouth for a guide, but considering that I spend 10 solitary hours with him each day, total silence makes me squirm. You simply never know what the guide is thinking – assuming he is in fact thinking. With Dern I was never sure.

One afternoon when the water was like glass and the only sound was the distant calling of a loon, I decided to initiate conversation once more.

"Where are you from, Dern?" I said, interrupting the otherwise placid moment.

"Newfoundland," he said.

"What's your hometown?"

"Nameless Cove," he answered.

"Are your parents native to Newfoundland and Nameless Cove?"

"Dunno, I never asked 'em," said Dern.

I pictured a family meal at Dern's house with his mom, dad and siblings all sitting around the table in silence. How could you not know where your parents are from, unless you didn't have parents? My conclusion was that conversation was not prized in Dern's house. After failing at conversation, I resigned to my solitary world of brook trout, which were every bit as chatty as Dern.

Bill Franklin of Dallas, Texas, was one of the five fishermen in our party. He was a towering figure, at least 6'2", and I imagine he tipped the scales somewhere around 275 pounds. Bill had hunted and fished all over the world, and as the former president of Browning Arms, he was a novice to nothing in the outdoor sporting world.

We swapped guides daily so by the end of our trip all of us would have fished with all the guides. On a day that I shall never forget, Ron, who seemed to be the head guide, guided Bill Franklin. Being a much smaller man than Bill, Ron and the outboard motor in the stern made a perfect counterbalance and subsequently the canoe was perfectly level from bow to stern.

That afternoon was memorable. As the sinking sun settled on the horizon under a clear evening sky, the huge green drake mayflies on the water were backlit, making them appear like tiny glowing chartreuse sailboats. The lake was dead calm. When a brookie sipped one of the drakes off the top, it made a pronounced dimple on the mirror surface.

That was our clue to cast our green drake imitations as close to the dimple as possible, which often inspired the trout to return to the surface for the facade.

Bill made a perfect cast and delivered his fly within inches of the rocking ringlets where the trout had just fed. His green drake imitation landed as gently as an airborne thistle. It had no more than settled on the surface when the audible slurp of a large brook trout bulged the surface and Bill's fly disappeared. He raised his rod to set the hook and there in the glorious golden hew of evening, it arched sharply under the strain of the big trout.

My canoe was nearby when Bill connected, so I started snapping photos. Eventually Bill brought the trout alongside the canoe, slipped his dip net under its sparkling body and lifted it into the canoe. Meanwhile, Ron, in the back of the canoe, began whooping and dancing, eventually dashing toward Bill with his right arm extended. Obviously he wanted to congratulate Bill on a job well done, and while the accolades were certainly in order, Ron was shifting the balance of the canoe with every step forward, until finally the motor was almost out of the water and the canoe was about to stand on its nose.

We were fishing in beautiful bright red 20-foot square-stern Chestnut canoes. They added a color of stark contrast against a world of deep blue water lined by verdant green timber. On open water, you could spot one a mile away.

Bill, realizing that he was about to be swamped, screamed at Ron to return to the stern. "Go back, you moron – go back!" he squalled. Ron retreated to his customary position in the stern, the canoe leveled out, and the day was saved. After Bill caught his breath he reminded Ron that verbal accolades would be more than sufficient. They could shake hands after they got out of the canoe.

Fifteen minutes later, Bill connected with another fine brookie. Ron, remaining aft, stood up to try to see the fish. He had a huge, long-handled net for occasions when the fisherman could not land the fish. Bill assured Ron that he had things under control. Not realizing that he was being photographed, Ron produced a bottle of beer, tipped it and drained it. Since Bill was sitting with his back to Ron, he had no idea what Ron was doing. While imbibing wasn't unpardonable, I knew it was strictly forbidden for the guides to drink while we were on the water. Ron knew it, too, but he just couldn't resist temptation.

I was running the motor drive all the while, so I have a perfect sequence of Bill fighting his fish from the bow while Ron was draining his bottle from the stern. It struck me funny. But what happened next made the sequence even more priceless. Ron seemed to have strained the beer through his kidneys in record time, and since Bill was still preoccupied with fighting his trout, Ron unzipped his pants and returned his beer to the dark waters of the Minipi.

After we returned to camp that evening, I told Ron about the spectacular pictures I had captured of him performing his guidely duties. He blushed a little; then he and the other guides found a bigger cache of bottles and began the celebration in earnest. When they were all feeling no pain, I asked if they could sing "I's the B'y," a 19th century Newfoundland fish boxing and gutting, net mending and light hauling song that was sung (and probably still is) at Fogo, Moreton's Harbour, Bona Vista and other Newfoundland fishing ports.

Shoulder to shoulder, arm in arm, they sang their hearts out as they danced a little jig and butted hips on cue, laughing open heartedly under a canopy of brilliant Labrador stars. It was hilarious and a perfect way to end a most amusing fishing adventure. I can think of no better way to conclude this chapter than to let you delve into the lyrics of "I's the B'y," and imagine five tipsy fishing guides performing it on the shores of the Minipi.

I's the B'y
Words & Music: Traditional

I's the b'y that builds the boat
And I's the b'y that sails her
I's the b'y that catches the fish
And brings them home to Liza
Hip yer partner, Sally Thibault

Hip yer partner, Sally Brown
Fogo, Twillingate, Moreton's Harbour
All around the circle!

Sods and rinds to cover your flake
Cake and tea for supper
Codfish in the spring o' the year
Fried in maggoty butter

I don't want your maggoty fish
They're no good for winter
I could buy as good as that
Down in Bonavista

I took Liza to a dance
As fast as she could travel
And every step that she did take
Was up to her knees in gravel

Susan White, she's out of sight
Her petticoat wants a border
Old Sam Oliver in the dark
He kissed her in the corner

CHAPTER 5

Flight Of The Trichoptera

IT WAS A GLORIOUS EVENING on the lower Bow River, east of Calgary, Alberta. As the sunset cast a molten bronze hew on the water, a cloud of caddis flies danced on the river's surface, enticing huge rainbow and brown trout into a feeding frenzy. The only sounds were the whistling of the prairie wind, the gurgling of the river and the slurping and slashing of big trout as they fed ravenously upon the swarming flies.

My brother John and I fished from the bank, our fly rods working frantically above the wallowing trout. It was the end of a perfect day of fishing, and as darkness fell, we were treated to a truly unsurpassed fly-fishing experience.

The beautiful picture lingers in my mind's eye. The only peculiar feature of that image is the red bandana I was wearing over my face. I looked like a misplaced bank robber out of some old western movie. I wore it so I could breathe without inhaling a mouthful of caddis flies. They were that thick.

If swarms of bugs bother you, you might find such a caddis hatch a little unnerving, but they are harmless little creatures. They don't sting or bite. They just swarm and skitter along the river's surface, and the trout go wild! Then for days after, you find caddis flies in all your clothing and fishing tackle. Small price to pay for the incredible trout fishing they produce when they hatch en masse!

I was in the midst of a back cast when one supersonic little fly came sailing along on the brisk prairie wind and was shot unexpectedly into my right ear. He arrived with such velocity that neither of us had time to respond before it was too late. When he came to the end of his last ride, he landed like a bullet against my eardrum. The net effect of his crash landing struck such severe pain to my eardrum that it literally knocked me off my feet. It was like being shot. Brother John peered inquisitively through the cloud as I writhed on my back in agony. I must have looked like a man possessed.

"Uh, what's wrong?" John asked reluctantly, spitting out a caddis fly or two.

"I got a caddis fly on my eardrum!" I gasped.

"Man, did you see the size of that brown that just rolled in front of me?" John asked with compassion as he dropped his fly into the swarm.

The captive fly was undoubtedly as concerned about our predicament as I was, but I was sure that I was in much greater pain. He would lie still for a moment and the pain would subside. About the time I thought I was back in control, he'd beat his wings against my tender eardrum and bring me back to my knees. The next few minutes offered the alternate entertainment of watching me trying to overcome the pain of my unexpected visitor long enough to make the proverbial "last cast" and then suddenly being knocked back to the ground by the fluttering of little wings. The pain created by the little bug was all out of proportion for his size.

Finally, when it was too dark to see, John and I climbed back into our Mackenzie boat and drifted the last two miles to the landing where I'd parked my truck. At last the little bug in my ear calmed down and was very still. Nonetheless, severe pain persisted. I was so debilitated that John had to drive the 25 miles back into Calgary.

As we drove along, John remembered the time a bug crawled into his ear. Like me, he was in great pain and feared that the insect might lay eggs, which would subsequently hatch into larva in his inner ear and then burrow into his brain. I identified with his concern.

"Well, didja get the bug out of your ear?" I asked.

"Yeah, I did," he replied thoughtfully. "You're never gonna believe how I did it."

"Well try me!" I pressed. "This is no time for secrets!"

As he began explaining his bizarre remedy, we pulled up to the first red light at the south end of town.

"Somebody told me that bugs were attracted to light," he began. "So I got the idea that if I went into a dark room and held a light up to my ear, the bug might just crawl toward it."

"So, did he?"

"Sure did," John replied, "Just slick as a whistle ... pretty soon here he came, out to that light. When he got all the way out I grabbed him and mashed him good and that was the end of that."

"Well, it's dark now, and I have a flashlight in my fly vest," I ventured. "Think that would work?"

"Don't see why it wouldn't," he shrugged. "It sure worked for me."

I found my little penlight, turned it on and stuck it in my right ear.

"Well, here goes," I said as the light turned green.

It wasn't until the light changed that I became aware of the car to my right, which had been stopped beside us at the red light. With the flashlight still in my ear, I glanced over my shoulder and realized that I was being watched. There were four people in that car, and every one of them was staring at the weirdo with the flashlight in his ear. I suppose my right ear was lit up like a Jack-O'-Lantern. I made a futile gesture to assure them that there was a very logical reason for the flashlight in my ear, but I could tell as they sped away shaking their heads that it wasn't convincing.

By now my inner ear was inflamed, and my eardrum throbbed every time my heart beat, which as I recall was about 73 times a minute. I had better sense than to wish my heart would stop beating, but I certainly would have settled for something about quarter speed.

It was 1 a.m. when I checked into emergency at Foothills Hospital. An hour later (slow night?), I was admitted to see the doctor. He was a lively little man in his 30s with the personality of a slug and the bedside manner of Attila the Hun. Though he was all business, I couldn't help but wonder if the ink was dry on his doctor's license. I had the distinct impression I was the first living patient to darken his door.

In truth, my personality was probably not at its bubbly best at that hour. I was in a world of hurt, in no mood for dumb experiments. Still, the doctor, after an initial examination of the ailing ear, came at me with a little stainless steel bar about 10 inches long. He called it a probe.

I'm no rocket scientist, but I knew that my ear canal was (A) not 10 inches deep, and (B) not straight. However, Dr. Slug, with one jarring thrust, attempted to redesign my ear canal to the opposite configuration of both A and B.

It felt like burning steel driving into my brain, and I involuntarily jumped from my stool and grabbed Dr. Slug by the arm, which was still attached to the hand that held the probe. "OOOOOH, THAT'S NEVER GONNA WORK!" I screeched. Oops – I also had the good doctor in a Half Nelson.

I released his arm, apologized and explained about the unique curve of my ear canal.

"Maybe we should just try to flush it out with water," he winced.

I nodded my agreement.

The doctor left to get the necessary equipment. I had seen this operation before. Fortunately, it is fairly painless and effective. Why hadn't we tried the flushing routine in the first place? I suppose some doctors are just born to probe first and flush later. In any case, while I was waiting for his return, I spotted the water fountain on the wall on the opposite side of the examination room. I was suddenly overcome with a scheme to totally discombobulate Dr. Slug. It wasn't really meanness; it was more along the lines of comic relief. I needed some relief about then.

I jumped off my stool, raced to the drinking fountain and filled my mouth with water, and returned to my stool, holding the water in my mouth. Presently Dr. Slug returned with a large syringe and a curved stainless steel pan. As expected, he instructed me to hold the pan below my ear while he squirted water into my ear with the syringe. I grunted and nodded my understanding.

The doctor lined up the syringe and squirted a stream of warm water into my ear canal. Simultaneously I squirted a similar stream of water out between my two front teeth. Upon seeing this, the doctor gasped and dropped his syringe on the floor. The horrified look on his face was that of a doctor about to lose a malpractice suit. I swallowed the remaining water and asked nonchalantly, "Did the bug come out, Doc?"

I pulled the little pan down from my ear and there floating in the bottom was a little brown caddis fly. He had paid the ultimate price for his opportunity to beat on my eardrum.

The astonished doctor leaned over and gazed into the pan, then looked up at me in utter bewilderment.

“Look here, Doc,” I said. “Congratulations! You got him out.”

“Exactly what is it?” the doctor asked rather weakly, obviously still concerned about the leak I had sprung.

“It looks like a size 14 Trichoptera to me,” I said.

“I’m sure it is,” he replied with a worried smile.

I handed him the pan, shook his hand and thanked him for his help. Then I walked out into the cool night air, leaving Dr. Slug with mouth agape, wondering what on earth had gone wrong.

What had I learned from the experience? It was simple. In addition to the bandana, I would add one set of earplugs. Whatever it takes to endure a caddis fly hatch.

CHAPTER 6

In Search of the Cassandra

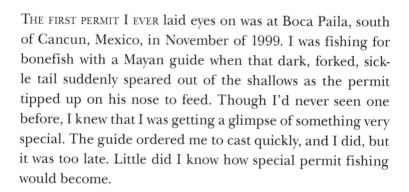

THE FIRST PERMIT I EVER laid eyes on was at Boca Paila, south of Cancun, Mexico, in November of 1999. I was fishing for bonefish with a Mayan guide when that dark, forked, sickle tail suddenly speared out of the shallows as the permit tipped up on his nose to feed. Though I'd never seen one before, I knew that I was getting a glimpse of something very special. The guide ordered me to cast quickly, and I did, but it was too late. Little did I know how special permit fishing would become.

Gary Sitton and I had taken our families to Cancun for a holiday. The Sittons and my kids and their spouses threw a surprise 30th anniversary party for my wife Sharleen and me. It just shows how long a marriage can last if you do enough fishing. While the rest of the gang frolicked in the ocean, Gary and I embarked on our long-planned fishing trip to the high seas. We had an armload of heavy-duty fly rods, and though neither of us was quite sure what to do with them out in the Caribbean, we were determined to find out. It was the off-season, so there would be no billfish, but perhaps some dorado or barracuda would be hanging around.

Gary had prearranged for the boat and captain with some agency in Dallas. We took a taxi to the marina where the boat and captain "Kuko" were supposed to be waiting only to find a few local commercial fishermen bringing in their catches of snapper – no sports fishing boat and no captain in sight.

"What's the name of our boat?" I asked.

Gary dug around until he found the contract.

"The Cassandra!" he announced.

So we walked the docks looking at boat names, but there was no Cassandra. I saw several baby tarpon swim out from under the dock, so I abandoned the search for the Cassandra long enough to cast to them, but they weren't interested.

"Well, let's go ask those fishermen if they know anything about the Cassandra," Gary suggested.

"I hope they speak some English. Don't know if my Spanish will stand the test of something that complicated," I admitted.

Gary approached and asked, "Do any of you speak English?"

The men stopped sorting fish and looked at Gary like three calves staring at a new gate.

"I think that means no," I offered.

Undaunted, Gary called on his rich Spanish vocabulary and said, "CASSANDRA!"

He pointed toward the boats for emphasis. "BOTA CASSANDRA," he exclaimed, waving and pointing. "BOTA NOMBRE CASSANDRA!"

I marveled at his fluency, as did the three Mexican fishermen, who by then had risen to their feet and were peering quizzically at the boats where Gary was pointing.

"DONDE CASSANDRA?" Gary continued in a very loud voice, which aids greatly in being understood by foreigners.

"Mmmmm," said the elder fisherman, looking thoughtfully toward the boats.

Communication at last!

"CASSANDRA!" Gary continued, optimistically.

"Si, Cassandra," muttered the old Mexican.

"He remembers the Cassandra," Gary said, "Now we're getting somewhere."

In the meantime, my son-in-law, Barry, had walked to the next marina to see if anyone there knew of the Cassandra. He returned with no news. "You guys finding out anything?" he asked. I pointed toward Gary and gave him a thumbs up.

"Gary speaks Spanish and has this thing under control," I said confidently.

Now the weathered fisherman was nodding and saying "Cassandra," while scratching his head, seemingly trying to remember where or when he last saw her. It was just a matter of time. The whole event just affirmed the value of knowing a second language.

"CASSANDRA!" Gary blurted jubilantly.

We waited with bated breath for the old man to make the connection. Finally, after much deliberation, he lifted his hands, shrugged his shoulders and muttered, "No hablo Ingles, señor."

That meant that either A) he couldn't understand English or B) Gary wasn't speaking loud enough. It turned out to be option "A."

The fishermen went back to sorting their snappers and we walked off the dock to see if we could find someone who really understood English. Gary handed me the contract and I began reading it. There in the box that noted the contact person with whom Gary had made the arrangements was the key: the word "Cassandra." Bingo: the search was over.

"Hey Sitton," I sneered. "You're never gonna believe this, but the Cassandra is not the name of the boat. It's the name of the lady you talked to at the agency when you booked the trip. It says right here that her name is Cassandra!"

Gary snatched the contract out of my hand, verified my observation, and we all sat down and had a good laugh. When we read a little farther down the page, we discovered that our boat (I've forgotten her actual name) was, in fact, supposed to be moored at that marina. As we walked along the dock, looking again for our vessel, a short Mexican man stepped out of the cabin of a big Bertrand.

"Mr. Seeton?" he inquired.

"Yes, I'm Sitton," Gary said, relieved.

"I will be your captain," the little man replied.

Gary glanced at the contract only to realize that this was a much larger boat than he had chartered, and this was not Captain Kuko. Gary quizzed the man about the change and found that the boat he had originally chartered had been damaged and taken back to the U.S. for repairs, along with the original American captain.

"This is an awful big boat and not really designed for fly fishing," Gary said with due concern.

"No fly fishing!" announced the captain.

While we were recoiling from that announcement, he added that for $800 per day he would not furnish lunch or beer. With amazingly few (but highly expressive) words, Gary explained that the charter was off. We grabbed a taxi back to the hotel and started over. The hotel concierge lined us up for the afternoon with a very accommodating captain, who, although not knowledgeable about fly fishing, was willing to try. And try we did, but to round out a perfectly impossible day, the seas were so rough we spent most of the time trying not to get pitched overboard. Finally we threw in the towel. On the way to shore, Barry caught one king mackerel while trolling with conventional tackle.

Our captain graciously gave us the name of a local man who owned a flats boat and guided fly fishermen. We managed to book him for the next four days.

We fished along the network of mangroves of Laguna Nichupte, right in front of hotel row, and caught small tarpon and snook, along with a few snapper and barracuda. After the first day on the flats, Gary initiated his customary "start earlier" campaign, asking the guide to pick us up at 6 a.m., instead of the usual 7:00. I kissed any hope of a full night's sleep goodbye.

The unknowing guide obliged and showed up at 6:00 as requested. Gary talked him into a 5 a.m. arrival the following morning. So, at 4:45, we were waiting on the dock. I wondered how in the world the guide would be able to cross the bay in his little skiff in pitch dark. Eventually, we heard the familiar hum of an outboard motor, followed by the faint red running lights of our skiff. Like a homing pigeon, the guide pulled up beside the dock and we jumped in. Another 30-minute boat ride found us in the maze of narrow canals lined with eerie black silhouettes of twisted mangrove roots and limbs.

As the first faint streak of pink slipped above the horizon, we could see the swirls of tarpon on the surface. I had taken a 10-pounder the previous morning, so Gary was up first. A nice fish porpoised 40 feet off the port bow, and Gary dropped his Blueback Deceiver right on the money – six feet ahead of it. A flash of silver greeted the fly as soon as it touched the water, and the morning stillness was shattered by a cartwheeling tarpon and Gary's laughter, signaling that all was well with the world. Fifteen minutes later he boated a 15-pounder.

It was our first venture into flats fishing, and we were hooked. My only regret was that Gary's "start earlier" campaign had accomplished what he predicted – a good tarpon at daybreak. I was hoping he'd catch a tarpon, but not until about 9 or 10 a.m. So much for future sleep.

Our guide suggested that we look into the bonefish at Boca Paila, just two hours south, so we called and were lucky enough to make a one-day booking.

A suburban arrived at the hotel at 6 a.m. and drove us to the lodge, via one hour of good pavement and another down a narrow, bumpy dirt road cut through the dense tropical jungle, complete with a military check stop in the middle of nowhere. It appeared that the soldiers (who looked like a uniformed drug ring themselves) were looking for contraband.

Boca Paila's lodge is strategically located on a sliver of sand separating the Caribbean Sea and a vast network of backwater flats. A narrow inlet, a stone's throw from the lodge, connects the Caribbean and the flats. While the area is renowned for bonefish, there are also good numbers of tarpon and permit, making the coveted salt water fly fishing grand slam possible. In addition, there are plenty of snook, barracuda, and snapper.

Gary and Barry shared a boat and guide while my son Darren and I shared another. At the end of the day, Darren and I had boated 23 bonefish, the largest of which was about four pounds. Gary and Barry had similar success. We tossed Crazy Charlies at the bones and they ate them like candy. Like all first-timers out for bonefish, we were amazed by their tenacity. Their fight was out of proportion for their size. At hookup they would streak out across the flats with sizzling runs, often 100 yards or more. Then, when we thought they were tiring and coming to the net, they'd do it all again.

You gotta love a fish like that. But after my first day of bone fishing, even as impressed as I was with their fight, what excited me most was seeing that permit. I distinctly remember the excitement in my guide's voice when he spotted that forked tail and hissed, "Permit, permit – cast, cast, cast!"

As we made the trip back to the hotel that night, Gary and I compared notes on our first ever day of flats fishing and concluded that, until then, we had been missing out on a most wonderful dimension of fly fishing. We couldn't wait to do it again.

At home, I became obsessed with researching flats fly fishing. Everywhere I turned, permit were held in highest esteem. It was obviously the Holy Grail of saltwater fly fishing, if not of all water. I read about spotting tailing fish and stalking into casting distance, the need for pinpoint casting accuracy, and about how after doing everything exactly right, the odds of the fish taking the fly were still extremely slim. It read like a chapter from a book on stalking trophy whitetails. I have devoted a goodly chunk of my life to that pursuit, so it had a familiar ring. Fly fishing for permit on coral or sand flats was obviously more hunting than fishing. Everything was the same except that in the end, you use a fly rod instead of a rifle or a bow. I have fly fished for everything from brown trout to sailfish, and I must confess that no fish ever intrigued me like a permit, especially considering that I had only seen one in my life and had caught none.

Though I had never met Jack Samson, former editor in chief of Field and Stream and editor of Fly-fishing & Tying Journal, his book, "Permit on a Fly" convinced me that permit would be my fish of a lifetime. I was never so sure of anything.

Samson noted that not so long ago, everyone who had caught a permit on a fly probably knew each other. The fraternity was that small. The fact that capable fishermen often spent years trying before they caught their first permit on a fly pointed to a supreme challenge, which made it even more appealing to me. In truth, this was still a young sport, pioneered by a faithful few and now waiting for Gary and me. It was an itch that had to be scratched.

My research pointed to Belize for the best odds for permit. Authorities agreed that the coral flats of the Caribbean, between the barrier reef and the mainland of Belize, were second to none in terms of numbers of permit. From my point of view it was purely a numbers game: the more fish in the area, the greater the chances to catch one. I figured that given enough opportunities, eventually I'd prevail against this legendary aquatic equivalent of a trophy white-tailed buck.

Finally, after reading everything I could get my hands on, I was convinced that Blue Horizon Lodge, on Northeast Cay south of Dangriga, was the place to start. Samson's book lavished some pretty heavy accolades on the Westby brothers, David and Lincoln, calling them the world's best permit guides.

I spent many years as a fishing and hunting guide and considered myself a cut above average with a fly rod, so I concluded that all I needed was for the world's best permit guide to point me to the fish and I'd handle the rest. I want to go on record and say that of all the guides I've fished or hunted with in my life, for everything from grayling to grizzlies, none have ever contributed more to my success than Lincoln Westby. But I'm getting ahead of myself.

I called Gary and advised him of my findings and conclusions about the commencement of our plunge into permit fishing, so we picked a week in May 2000. We booked the trip with Blue Horizon Lodge through the Fly Shop in Redding, Calif. The young man I spoke with said he'd been there and that we should expect to cast to an average of 15 permit per day. He admitted that neither he nor anyone else in his party actually landed a permit, although they hooked a couple.

Initially I was stunned by the lack of success he reported, but then reasoned that perhaps they were not good casters, which I knew from my own guiding experience was the reason most fly fishermen fail. In six days of fishing to 15 fish per day, I assumed that I'd cast to at least 90 permit. I remember thinking: "I've never cast to 90 of anything, no matter how smart or wary, without catching them – and usually lots of them."

In retrospect it's funny how blindly optimistic one can be about something with which he has had absolutely no experience. Sure, I had never cast to 90 fish I couldn't catch, but I had also never cast to a permit. If I had, I would have realized why the average length of time for fly fishermen, from beginning to landing their first permit, is seven years! I sent Samson's book to Gary and it had the same effect on him. I have no idea if Jack Samson could catch a permit in a washtub, but of this I am sure: He motivated me with his writing as few writers have. For the remaining several months before our trip, Gary and I bought new tackle and all the known gear required for flats fishing. We both bought 10-weight rods and reels primarily for the advantage of the heavier line for casting in windy conditions. It turned out to be a very wise choice. In addition, I tied a footlocker full of crab patterns.

We finally met in Dallas and flew to Belize City, then squeezed into a little twin-engine puddle jumper for the 20-minute hop to Dangriga. A young man named Tyrone drove us the final 35 miles to the little coastal town of Hopkins. It was late evening when we arrived at the dead end of a narrow dirt road on the banks of the Sittee River. To say it was rural would be an understatement. Since our boat was not waiting for us as planned, Tyrone made a call to find out why. "No problem," he announced as he clicked off his cell phone. "Your boat will be here very soon."

We were relieved to hear that, but nearly two hours later said relief waned. "Where does the guy live that's bringing the boat?" I asked.

"In Hopkins," Tyrone replied.

"You mean right there in the little town we just passed to get here?"

"Yes," he nodded.

"Do you know where he lives?"

"Yes," he nodded once more.

"Well then, I suggest that we unload our gear on the bank and you drive back to Hopkins and find out what's happened to him. Gary and I will stay here and keep an eye on our stuff 'til you get back."

And with that we broke the cardinal rule of foreign outdoor adventures: Never let the vehicle out of your sight until you arrive at your destination!

Like dummies we dumped our gear and Tyrone drove away, leaving us in a cloud of mosquitoes whose collective whine rivaled that of a jet engine. As we slapped ourselves silly, flailing against the endless barrage of bloodsuckers, we couldn't help wishing we had taken the insect repellent listed on our "what to bring" list more seriously. Between us we had not a drop of repellent, and the mosquitoes knew it.

As darkness fell we had a sinking feeling that Tyrone had jumped ship and left us there as living sacrifices to the gods of the stupid and the gullible, an honor for which we were both feeling profoundly over-qualified. There we were, standing in the dark, Dumb and Dumber, with no idea where we were or where we would go if Tyrone turned out to be a scoundrel. Hopkins was the only place we could find and that had slightly less appeal than being eaten alive by the mosquitoes.

"So what if the guy in the boat does show up?" Gary snorted, as he slapped a big one on the side of his head. "Didn't Tyrone say we couldn't travel by boat after dark? From where I'm standing, Thorny, it's darker than the inside of a cow!"

"What a bleak thought," I replied. "You don't suppose they've got a vacant double room at the Hopkins Hilton? This is their busy season, you know ... and us with no reservations."

Finally, in the distance, a single headlight bounced onto the little dirt road where we'd seen Tyrone disappear an hour earlier. Things were looking up, or so it seemed. Tyrone pulled up and announced that he had found another boat and driver. The new and improved transportation would be coming up the river any minute. Forty-five minutes later, standing in coal-black darkness, straining our eyes and ears and swatting mosquitoes, we heard the faint whine of an outboard motor out on the Sittee. Eventually, the boat droned closer, finally arriving at the appointed spot on the bank. It was so dark I could barely recognize the shape of the long narrow craft, even thought it was only a few feet away.

"This is Floyd, your new boat driver," announced Tyrone, as the stranger stepped out on the bank. We shook hands and started loading our gear.

"I thought Tyrone said we couldn't make this trip in the dark," Gary said nervously.

"Oh, we'll make it, no problem," Floyd answered plainly.

"How long is the trip?" I asked.

"Forty-five minutes to an hour," Floyd said, "depending on how rough it is on the water."

Once our gear was stowed, Gary and I took our positions in the boat's middle seat and Tyrone pushed us into the river.

"Good luck," he said, as we were swallowed by the night. We could not see the water or the bank, much less determine our direction, but Floyd's instincts prevailed. I held my breath, fully expecting to slam into the bank at any moment, whereupon a gaggle of jaguars would be anxiously awaiting my arrival. But miraculously we steamed out of the mouth of the Sittee and into the heaving Caribbean.

The water was rough due to high winds, so we were soon drenched by the waves. All the while Floyd sang and whistled, just out of tune enough to keep our teeth on edge. He seemed altogether too cheerful. There we were without compass or light, crashing along through rough seas in a glorified rowboat, wondering if we had finally bitten off more fishing adventure than we could chew. Floyd was singing and whistling like he had won the lottery.

Gary and I, totally absorbed by our thoughts and reservations, did not speak for 30 minutes. Finally I saw the blue glow of Gary's wristwatch as he checked our elapsed travel time. "Thirty minutes," he announced skeptically. The longest thirty minutes of my life.

My imagination was working a double shift. "This guy's going to take us out here in the middle of the sea, shoot us, grab our wallets and dump us overboard, and no one will ever know what happened to us," I thought. "How could we have made such a mistake and let ourselves be so foolishly trusting? But other people must have done this. We can't be the only ones, and there have been no reports of missing permit fishermen," my fearful and rational mind argued.

Somewhere between imagining myself as a shark's dinner and telling myself this was really no big deal, I saw a light in the distance. It was a narrow beam that swung in an arc like a miniature lighthouse beacon. "Did you see that light?" Gary and I chimed in unison.

Gary's wristwatch glowed once more. "It's been 45 minutes," he announced with newfound hope. I sighed, deeply relieved. Then the light swung back and forth ahead of us again. I could feel the boat swing around in the waves, nosing toward the little beacon. For the first time in several hours I was willing to believe that all was well and that this was just a little test of nerves to determine whether or not we were really cut out for permit fishing. Fifteen minutes later we arrived at the dock on Northeast Cay, home of Blue Horizon Lodge. It was, in fact, just a day in the life of travel in Central America – no sinister plots, no getting fed to sharks. I remembered the old saying that "getting there is half the fun."

Lincoln Westby was waiting on the dock to meet us. He had provided the guiding beacon with his flashlight. I had never been so happy to meet a man in my life!

The next morning at dawn, our skiff backed away from the dock and headed for the surrounding coral reefs, seemingly as numerous as the stars. Permit were scarce and the few we saw were afraid of their own shadows. Or should I say, lack of shadows. An unsettled weather pattern had moved into the area with strong, ever-changing winds, heavy overcast and unusually low tides – a combination that kept the permit at bay.

Floyd, who was still our guide, explained that permit relax in clear, sunny weather when shadows on the water can be seen clearly and interpreted as danger, i.e. pelicans, frigate birds, ospreys and such, which bombard fish from on high. At the sight of a passing shadow, permit simply scurry off the flats and into deep water. However, when overcast conditions prevail, and there are no shadows, only a brave few permit approach the flats, and they are so wary that they are almost impossible to approach. Such was our fate for the first four days of our five-day trip. On the fourth day I finally made my first cast to a tailing permit. It was too long and when the line landed on the water above him, he exploded off the flats. In those same four days, Gary never had a single opportunity.

On what was supposed to be our fifth and final fishing day, Lincoln guided us for the first time. The weather settled temporarily and produced calm winds and a bluebird sky. The change was dramatic. For the first time we were able to see the full spectrum of the blue waters in the Caribbean. It was breathtakingly beautiful. In addition, the previous vacant flats held permit. Lincoln announced that he had the next four days free due to a party's last-minute cancellation, so we booked an additional three days, with him as guide. Gary and I took turns casting with each new fish. Lincoln's patient teaching was extremely beneficial and served to illustrate how little we actually knew.

I had read that you must cast your fly well ahead of the feeding permit and hope he discovers it and grabs it. That might may be an acceptable routine on sandy flats with higher visibility, or where permit are really on the move, but certainly not to tailing fish on the coral reefs of Belize.

Lincoln instructed us to drop the fly right on the nose of tailing permit, then quickly strip all the slack out of the line, and if he so commanded, to strip-set the hook quickly and firmly. It was not all that complicated in theory, but in practice it was another matter. I soon discovered that strip setting was a hurdle I might never clear. Thirty years of fly fishing for trout had so ingrained striking by raising my rod tip that it was as involuntary as blinking my eyes. Time and again, though I tried to force myself not to raise my rod tip, I did it anyway, and each time forfeited my chance at a willing permit.

On that day it seemed that every time it was my turn to cast, the opportunity was perfect. When it was Gary's turn, the opportunity would be marginal at best. But that was the luck of the draw.

Once, three permit were tailing together within easy range. Lincoln and I slipped out of the skiff and crept into casting position. My cast was perfect and as I was easing the slack out of my line, I felt a quick snap. I struck, only to realize that a small yellowtail snapper had grabbed my fly before the permit could get to it. I thought my heart would explode when I felt the fish take, and words can't describe my disappointment when I realized it was a snapper.

Thirty minutes later Lincoln poled the skiff up on a small flat, on the tail of a mangrove-covered cay. He told us there were three permit that fed there regularly on the rising tide. He had guided countless fishermen to these same three fish over a three-year period, yet no one had hooked a single fish.

As advertised, there were three sickle-blade tails waving above the water as the grand fishes foraged eagerly upon the coral reef in the sunshine. Lincoln eased the skiff into position and ordered me to take my shot from the bow. My cast was good. "Strip out the slack," he ordered.

I obliged.

"Move it a little!" he said, which I did. Suddenly, feeling a sharp tug, I struck like an over-wound coil spring. When I did, I snatched a small barracuda completely out of the water. "Strip him away from the permit!" Lincoln shouted. I was stripping for all I was worth when my line went slack, thanks to the 'cuda's razorblade teeth. He had bitten through my tippet and relieved me of my fly. Again I thought my heart would stop. I could hardly believe my luck. Two perfect opportunities, both ruined by imposters.

The permit were still tailing, so I told Gary to take over. He stripped off line and made a dandy cast right into the fray. His fly barely touched the water before a permit hit the fly so hard that he hooked himself. Gary just hung on and howled with ecstasy while the permit headed for deep water with a blistering run, sizzling deep into his backing. Everything was perfect.

Gary was about to be inducted into that small fraternity of souls who have caught fly fishing's Holy Grail. After about 15 minutes the fish began to tire. His chrome flanks glistened and flashed from the deep. Lincoln leaned over the gunnels and prepared to tail it with his bare hand.

"How big is he?" Gary asked.

"He's 18 to 20 pounds," Lincoln replied, grinning like a proud father.

It looked as big as a garbage can lid, flashing and pumping against Gary's rod. Now only the leader remained between the tip of his rod and his first permit.

"Just keep tension on him," Lincoln said. "When he lays over on his side, I'll land him."

The great fish finally rolled over on his side, but apparently he saw something he didn't like. He suddenly tipped his nose down and lunged into the endless blue below the boat. Suddenly Gary's rod tip sprung up straight. The fish was gone. "Nooooooooo," Gary groaned in agony as Lincoln and I stood silently, almost afraid to speak.

Gary lifted his rod and grabbed his leader. At the end was the telltale sight of a twisted pigtail of monofilament, spelling out the horrible truth. The leader had not broken. His clinch knot had slipped.

It's the little stuff that kills you in permit fishing. Lincoln recommended that in the future we leave an eighth of an inch of excess when we clipped our leaders after tying on a fly. That way the tension wouldn't pull the knot apart. He would get no argument from us.

I had never felt so sorry for anyone in my life. As the saying goes, "Close only counts in horseshoes and hand grenades." The old adage certainly applies to permit fishing.

That day was by far the best of that first trip, in terms of tailing fish and good casting opportunities, but by the next day the unsettled weather pattern returned, along with rain and overcast skies that made the few permit very skittish. I cast to several, but the only one that accepted my offering was lost to my continued inability to strip-strike. No mattered how

I tried, when the fish took, my rod tip sprang up like it was spring loaded.

I not only missed a good permit, but I also missed my chance at a huge tarpon for the same reason. Until I overcame my mental block and began to strip set the hook, I was wasting everyone's time. When we headed back into the lodge for lunch, I was feeling pretty disgusted. Overcoming my rod-striking nemesis was the most difficult thing I'd encountered since taking up the fly rod some 30 years earlier.

After lunch, Gary took a siesta and I sat on the porch of our cabin and pondered my striking dilemma. Somehow I was going to have to force my mind to alter its programmed response to a striking fish. I decided to try visualization. For two hours I sat there with my eyes closed, envisioning the sight of permit tipping up and grabbing my fly. Then I envisioned myself yarding back on the line with my stripping hand, leaving my rod pointed straight at the fish. I was still going when Gary walked out and announced it was time to catch the rising tide. I took a deep breath, hoping my mental exercise would make a difference.

Late in the afternoon, under blustery, overcast skies, Lincoln spotted a small school of permit feeding on the edge of a coral reef, only a few yards from deep water. The tides were running very low, often not bringing in enough water to allow the permit to move up on top of the flats, so they were hanging along the edges. I followed Lincoln out of the skiff and when we were positioned right, he told me to take my shot. I dropped my little self-tied, nickel-sized, green crab pattern ahead of the tailing permit.

"Strip it slowly!" Lincoln whispered. I did, and with each strip I spoke directly to the tip of my wayward fly rod. "Stay down, stay down, stay down," I commanded, as if it were some unruly puppy with a bad jumping habit. At that point I would have done anything to overcome my mental block, notwithstanding talking to myself, my fly rod, and anything else that would listen. As I moved the crab slowly on a tight line, I felt a sharp tick. To my amazement, I struck hard with my stripping hand. When I did, I felt the surge of power of an alarmed and well-hooked permit vibrating through my line.

"You got him!" Lincoln cheered as the fished bolted for the blue. Initially the feeling was surreal, as if a wonderful dream. But reality came thundering as the permit screamed backing off my reel. Lincoln hurried me toward the skiff so we could follow. In seconds we were back in the skiff in deep water. The permit fought with spectacular power. I had heard stories about how strong they were, and I was delighted to find that they had not been exaggerated. This fish was stronger than an acre of garlic!

Fortunately, since he had been feeding at the edge of the reef, instead of on top of it, his run for deep water didn't take him through the myriad coral heads that so often end the contest. But a few minutes into the fight, the permit concluded that his best hope for escape was back on the reef, so he left the deep and headed right back into the shallows where I had hooked him. He pumped downward toward the colorful, razor sharp coral formations, trying to grind the fly off against them.

I put all the pressure my leader would bear and eventually managed to stop him and force him back into deeper water. Twice more he headed back for the coral, but each time I managed to turn him. I was never so glad to have used a leader with 16-pound test tippet. I don't think I could have stopped him with anything lighter. And this wasn't a large fish. I couldn't imagine how I would have handled a 20- to 30-pounder in those conditions.

Finally, after a furious 15-minute battle, the fish lay over on his side beside the skiff and Lincoln's experienced hands pulled him into the boat. It was approximately 12 to 13 pounds, not particularly big by Belize standards, but it was the finest trophy of my career. It was a rare privilege to hold such a prize in my hands – to see the Holy Grail so still and vulnerable.

Oddly, for a fish that fights so valiantly, once tailed, permit surrender completely without so much as a flip of the tail. It might sound strange, but the fish appeared to have an unusually expressive face. Perhaps it was in his eyes, but he looked shy and embarrassed. Except for a slight touch of pale yellow on his under belly, he was chrome-plated from nose to tail. We devoted a couple rolls of film to the occasion and then released the grand fish. I had done it in spite of myself, and equal to my delight in actually catching my first permit on a fly was my delight with overcoming my rod-striking problem. I took additional delight in the fact that I caught the fish on an original deep green, nickel-sized crab pattern that I had tied especially for the occasion. Finally I felt like I had a chance to play the game as it must be played. One thing was certain: fly fishing would never be the same.

That was the one and only permit that we landed in our eight days of fishing. We had come during bad weather and bad tides, and somehow each of us had hooked a permit, so we were encouraged. It takes a certain mindset to fish for eight days, knowing full well that you might not catch a single fish, and yet somehow still cherish every minute of it. It's not for everyone.

I doubt there is much middle ground among fly fishermen where permit are concerned. Either they will frustrate you to the point that you never want to see another coral flat or they will allure you to the point of obsession. Gary and I have fallen squarely into the latter category. One thing became abundantly clear on our maiden permit voyage: If you have to catch a fish to justify your time and effort, then you're definitely not cut out for permit fishing. This chapter would be lacking if I failed to share one amazing incident that clearly illustrates why permit have such a reputation for being hard to catch even when the fisherman does everything right. On the last day, Lincoln spotted three tailing permit feeding together about 100 yards from the boat. It was my turn to cast, so Lincoln and I slid quietly over the gunnels into the knee-deep waters and Gary held the boat. When we were within 50 yards, Lincoln stopped to study the situation. We were watching the fish intently when one broke ranks and swam directly toward us, stopping at about 40 feet, facing us. "Don't move," Lincoln whispered. "He's coming to see what we are."

"Give me a break," I thought. "Don't tell me this is a scout coming to investigate two statuesque figures standing in the water." I know it makes some sportsmen feel better when they attribute human reasoning abilities to their quarry. Then when they prevail over the supposed "super intelligent" creatures they pursue, they can take a little more credit. But c'mon, this was a fish. I wasn't prepared to believe this crab eater was capable of complex reasoning.

He sat on the bottom, pointed our way, for about 15 seconds, and then turned back toward the other two. "He's going back to tell them we're here," Lincoln reported.

I silently scoffed at the notion.

As soon as the "scout" fish reached the other two, they seemed to get in a huddle for a split second, and then they streaked into the deep blue. Was it coincidence that they fled with such haste? For the first time I began to question my own resolve about the reasoning ability of fish. Lincoln's explanation seemed far-fetched, but I had no better explanation for what I had just witnessed. Why had that single fish broken ranks, why did it swim directly toward us, why did it stop, facing us, and what communication actually took place when it returned and the three fish huddled before leaving the flat like scalded cats? The questions outnumbered the answers. Maybe Lincoln was right. No stinking wonder permit are so hard to catch.

Epilogue

Of the 70-something photos taken when I caught my permit, Gary managed to get both the fish and I in two of them. His average is definitely getting better, but he's not ready to apply at National Geographic just yet.

CHAPTER 7

The Wake

THE GOOD REVEREND WHITE AND I stood in solemn silence in the boathouse, beside the body of the deceased. A heavy cloud of burden covered James like a blanket. He was responsible for the accident, although taking a life was the last thing he meant to do. No malice, no premeditation on his part ... it was simply an accident that couldn't be helped.

We'd seen the whole thing. James made every effort to save the victim's life, including a valiant mouth-to-mouth resuscitation effort, but it was to no avail. Everything that could have been done had been tried. Now James stood with his head slumped forward, chin against his chest. His eyes, like leaking flood gates, barely held back the ocean of agony that dripped slowly down his cheeks.

Words were useless now, incapable of reaching the depths of his sorrow. The silence was so intense that we dared not try to speak. I laid a helpless hand upon James' shoulder in a feeble effort to console him. He shook his head and whispered, "God knows I wish I could bring him back." Reverend White nodded his understanding without lifting his head.

Soon the women came in to view the body. James' wife Betty offered her condolences: "Big ol' sucker, wasn't he?"

My wife Sharleen and Reverend White's wife agreed and allowed that it was an awful shame about his passing.

Soon the women left, and we three men remained, eyes transfixed on the body of the deceased. Now a question loomed larger than life. What would be done with the body?

I knew that Reverend White secretly wanted to take it home and put it in his freezer, but he never would have asked. It would have been indiscreet under the circumstances. I thought we might consider performing a water burial, since that's where he died. Or perhaps James would want to have the body preserved for later viewing. In any case the decision was strictly James', so Reverend White and I remained silent, waiting for him to speak.

"Well, I guess there's nothing more we can do," James finally sighed. We nodded in nervous agreement. The question was about to surface.

"Whaddaya think we oughta do with him?" James asked at last. "Y'all might as well take him home and eat him."

Reverend White and I feigned an initial polite refusal, but James insisted. So, with a sincere sense of duty to the bereaved, we agreed to take the body off his hands.

James walked out of the boathouse, and the good Reverend and I leapt on the body with filleting knives and rendered the 9-pound bass into two delicious fillets. How rare the opportunity to actually make a meal out of one of James' pets! How many bass had we caught, drooled over, and returned to the lake, in respect for James' personal and intimate relationship with each and every one of the quarter million bass in his lake? How many times had we envisioned bass fillets rolled in cornmeal and fried with hush puppies?

And how many times had we dreaded the thought of being responsible for injury or death of one of those sacred creatures? This was catch-and-release fishing only, with no exceptions. Purposely killing one of James' bass is tantamount to the unpardonable sin. Accidentally killing one could even result in being banished from the kingdom. How ironic that James himself, the chief protector of his private herd of bass, foul-hooked the huge 9-pound trophy that was now destined for the deep fryer. It was ironic to say the least, and delicious to say the most.

However, we never bring up the subject in James' presence. Somehow it seems tasteless to talk about eating one's dear friend's pets in his presence. When the 9-pounder is mentioned, both Reverend White and I assume the necessary solemn expression and shake our bowed heads with our deepest and most bogus remorse.

Perhaps Betty's words spoken at the wake were the most fitting: "Big ol' sucker, wasn't he?"

CHAPTER 8

Moose on the Rocks

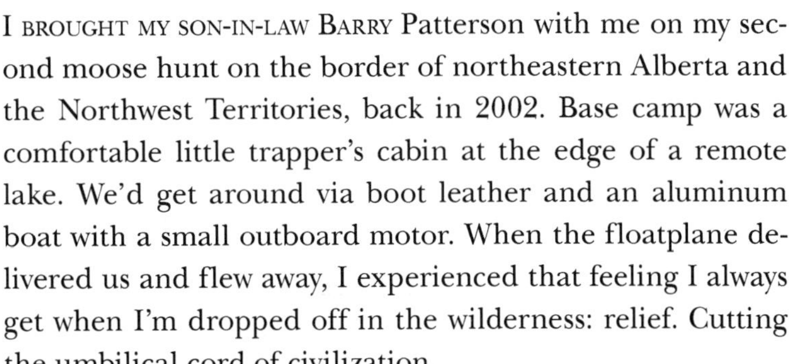

I BROUGHT MY SON-IN-LAW BARRY Patterson with me on my second moose hunt on the border of northeastern Alberta and the Northwest Territories, back in 2002. Base camp was a comfortable little trapper's cabin at the edge of a remote lake. We'd get around via boot leather and an aluminum boat with a small outboard motor. When the floatplane delivered us and flew away, I experienced that feeling I always get when I'm dropped off in the wilderness: relief. Cutting the umbilical cord of civilization.

Out there, peace and quiet fall over me like a warm blanket. I wonder if civilization is aptly named since the wilderness often seems far more civil than the rat race. A man can think uninterrupted thoughts until he decides to change them. The phone doesn't ring. There is no TV. There is just solitude. No trash on the streets because there are no streets. No thundering bass from an ear-splitting rap song in the car ahead of you. There are no cars. The world is clean out there where almost nobody goes. Yet the wilderness can be tough. One must prepare for Mother Nature. She can be a friend one day and a murderer the next.

Barry had never been on a moose hunt. To me, it was all about him getting a moose. I have toted many a slobber nose out of the muskeg in my day. Nothing would have made me happier than for Barry to experience the awe of standing over a 1,200-pound creature and wondering, "What the hell do I do now?"

That's what every moose hunter wonders when he bags his first. Any way you slice it, a moose equals much sweat and blood.

Our outfitter had picked this lake for us because of all the moose the trapper had seen during the summer. However, the lake was located in the Laurentian Shield, which is basically solid granite. The aquatic vegetation that had attracted the moose to the shore in the summer was long gone when we got there. Within a day or two, it was clear to me that no moose were around. Our high hopes for an encounter with Alces alces were tempering.

We searched for and called to moose to no avail. In fact, we named our remote body of water "Lake Devoid" for its lack of life forms, besides a few spruce grouse and pine squirrels.

Boredom turned to excitement one afternoon when Barry spotted a black bear across the lake. This was a welcome change from sitting in the cabin drinking coffee! We jumped into the little boat and zipped closer to where the bear was seen on a granite outcropping. Cautiously, we climbed up the downwind side of the granite so it wouldn't get our wind. In spite of our stealthy efforts, though, there was no bear in sight. We spread out 50 feet apart and edged slowly into timber. After covering the area thoroughly, we concluded that the bear had gone on its way, perhaps even to a nearby den. It was early October, so this stood to reason. Black bears typically den up by mid October at that latitude.

I'd brought a varmint call with me – the kind that sounds like a squealing rabbit. Over the years I had called in several black bears with it. I figured it was worth a try if the bear we were hunting was within earshot. After about 10 minutes of calling, listening and watching for the bear, Barry waved at me. He was trying to signal that he thought he'd heard a moose in the water below us. We crept toward the edge of the mountain of granite, hoping to see the lakeshore below us, but the thick spruce at the lake's edge hampered our view.

I walked to the top of a precipice overlooking a ravine below me, hoping for a better view. As I stepped to the edge, the soles of my rubber boots slipped forward on soggy rain-soaked lichens. Before I could think, I plummeted downward through a sheer boulder chute. My body ricocheted from one rock to another as I gained speed and momentum. Each boulder bounced me brutally in a new direction until, at the bottom of the 40-foot chute, I landed on my back on a huge egg-shaped rock.

There was a sharp cracking sound in the landing that I knew was bone. The pain was so overwhelming that at first I couldn't even identify its source. The landing knocked the breath out of me so hard that I thought I would suffocate. Poor Barry was watching the calamity from above. He admitted later that he was pretty sure I was a dead man. I must say that a similar thought crossed my mind several times on the way down.

Eventually I was able to catch my breath in short spurts. I was unsure of the extent of the damage, but the loud crack seemed to have come from my back. I assumed it was broken. But my fingers and toes moved on demand. Then my feet moved. Relief flooded me as I realized I was not paralyzed – at least not yet. That momentary fear of being paralyzed scared me worse than the fear of death.

I knew I couldn't stay on those cold granite boulders. I yelled to Barry to climb down, find the boat and get as close to me as he could. I think he was pretty happy to know he wasn't going to have to quarter me and haul my cold carcass back to camp.

The sound of the little outboard motor was sweet to my ears. Rolling on to my side, I felt an excruciating pain that took my breath once more. I could move slowly but with pain like I'd never known. Eventually I rose to my feet and cautiously navigated the final 50 yards to shore, where the boat was waiting. In what felt like slow motion, I climbed in and eased myself down to the plank boat seat. Though the pain seemed to be centralized in my back, I assumed that I had broken ribs but nothing else.

The climb from the boat to the cabin was a marathon. Once inside I just wanted to lie down. My sleeping bag was spread out on a foam mattress on the floor, which presented a new challenge. I had to drop to my knees and ease myself down on one side, then roll over on my back. I accomplished this with numerous involuntary shrieks, groans and panting. If I lay completely still on my back, the pain was minimal. But I didn't want to move. I didn't even want to blink.

The need to be perfectly still of course brought on coughing spells and sneezing, both of which felt like being stabbed in the back. A hiccup or a sneeze was more terrifying than the gallows, yet Barry and the guide thought I'd feel better if they made me laugh. I begged for mercy.

At long last, the floatplane landed just to check on us and see how the hunt was progressing. The pilot was bewildered to find me on the floor, gasping for a plane ride to the nearest doctor. I left my gear and my comrades behind and flew back to Fort Smith, Northwest Territories, where I was taken to the emergency room. The doctor greeted me with obvious apprehension. I told him what had happened. "Oh, you just broke a few ribs," he advised.

"Shouldn't I get an x-ray?" I asked

"No, I'll just tape you up until you get home. Then you can have your doctor take a look at you."

His passé approach wasn't comforting. It was obvious that he didn't want any part of this wounded American. The fact that he didn't x-ray me convinced me that he was either afraid of not getting paid or he feared a lawsuit in case he botched things.

I had three more days of trying not to cough or sneeze before my flight back to Edmonton and then a connection to my plane back to Montgomery, Ala., which was home at the time.

The x-rays showed that I had indeed broken ribs where they connect to the spine. It took a while to recover.

Looking back, I bear in mind that rubber boots and wet lichen-covered granite make for very tricky walking, even on level ground. So if you see wet lichens lining the edge of a granite rock, don't even think about. I am lucky to be alive.

I was invited to hunt moose with that same outfitter a couple of years later, but considering what had gone down, I respectfully declined. There are some places a man simply should not go.

CHAPTER 9

Airag, Anyone?

AFTER A DAY OF HOPPING my way through an Altai boulder field, higher than 12,000 feet, I was finished. And delirious. My legs were like rubber. I saw a few bones strewn among the rocks but no rams. Heck, those bones might have belonged to a former sheep hunter who made the same mistake. My Mongolian comrades kept assuring me that at any moment we would locate the Argali ram of my dreams. I knew something was dreadfully wrong when we spent the better part of an hour crawling on our bellies, sneaking up on a grand old ram that turned out to be another boulder. I didn't realize it then, but I was suffering from altitude sickness. (Later, a mountain climber would tell me that it takes the human body three full days to adjust to such extreme elevation changes before one can function as normal. Had I known that, I would have laid low for the first three days.) In the meantime I was dying on my feet, determined to at least die trying. After all, I had traveled halfway around the world for this hunt, but it seemed that a lot of money had been wasted on the return portion of my ticket. As our hunting party – my interpreter, my guide and my horseman (although we were on foot) and I – stood at the edge of the world's longest boulder field, looking down the endless valley, all was solemn and silent. Something was wrong.

"What's the matter?" I whispered to Alton, my interpreter. He turned to the guide and conveyed my question. After a few minutes of chatter, he came back with the terrifying truth.

"The jeep isn't where it's supposed to be," he said cheerfully. I knew what that meant. There had been a snafu in communications. The driver for our party had agreed to rendezvous with us at this point, and for some reason he wasn't there.

Well, where was he?

I had spent the day concentrating as hard as I could, trying to get my feet to cooperate with my mind. In my exhaustion, my feet seemed to operate in total independence. The boulders were huge. I could take two or three cautious steps before having to jump over a crevice to the next. I was afraid that one of my free-flying feet would send me down a dark hole to become a pile of bleached bones. In some ways that didn't sound so bad ... especially if I was expected to turn around now and retrace the last 10 hours of my journey.

"How far have we hopped?" I asked Alton.

Again he conferred with the guide. "Thirty kilometers," came his casual reply.

"No wonder I'm so beat," I thought. In my heart I knew I wasn't going to do any more boulders that day. Three or four miles down the grassy valley were three little white dots, which I knew were the yurts (a Mongolian tent, pronounced "ger") of some shepherds or herdsmen. I didn't speak Mongolian and I had no idea who lived in those little yurts, but I was sure they'd be pleased to make my acquaintance. "I'm going down there," I announced. "I don't know where the jeep went and I'm not hopping to my imminent death to find it, so if you need me, I'll be down there."

And with that I started down the valley. Happily Alton joined me, announcing that the others were going to look for the jeep. The estimated three or four miles turned out to be six or seven. Everything in Mongolia's High Altai Mountains is farther away than it looks. Even at that, it was downhill all the way with no boulders! At last we arrived at the yurts. As is typical of rural Mongolia, the women were out tending the yaks and milking the goats. Alton introduced himself and explained that we just happened to be in the neighborhood, so we thought we'd drop by. The women did a bit of yelling and soon the man of the yurt stepped outside. He was something of a giant, as Mongolians go ... about six feet tall. I estimated he'd tip the scales at 300 pounds. He was smiling and seemed happy to see us. We were immediately invited in and the atmosphere turned somewhat festive. Alton explained that I wasn't local, which I think he'd already figured out. The host welcomed me and bid me squat with him at his table, which was all of 10 inches high. How those Mongolians can squat. There were no chairs so squat it was.

Soon the lady of the yurt emerged with a large wooden bowl and set it on the table. Our host removed the cloth that covered the bowl, and then he and Alton cooed in unison as they gazed with delight at the contents. To me it looked like a bowl of milk. And it was ... sort of. The big man picked up a ladle and began dipping the white liquid high above the bowl, pouring it back, and then dipping it again. He and Alton were cackling with delight. I had never seen two grown men so worked up over a bowl of milk before. My host looked at me with a wicked grin, nodding as if to seek my approval. To be polite I grinned and nodded back, which obviously pleased him even more. The more we grinned and nodded at one another, the more he and Alton squealed with delight. Pretty soon we were all squatting there in near hysteria while the big Mongolian dipped himself into oblivion.

I had no idea what we were doing, but I knew it was something very special. A full-blown celebration. I was impressed with this guy's hospitable nature. Then the woman of the yurt set three glass bowls on the table. Our host dipped up the stuff in the big bowl and poured each of the three smaller bowls brim-full. He rested his ladle and presented both

Alton and me with a bowl of the white stuff. The atmosphere in the yurt was suddenly quiet and intense, as if something spectacular was about to happen.

"What is this stuff?" I whispered to Alton.

"It is our national drink," he replied politely.

"What's it called?" I asked.

"We call it Airag," he said. "It is the favorite drink of Mongolia."

Our host lifted his bowl in a toasting gesture. Then he and Alton tilted their bowls up and drained them in one gulp. I watched in amazement and then took a healthy swig, hoping to be like one of the boys. As the Airag hit my taste buds, my entire body heaved. The first gulp danced around in my throat as if looking for somewhere else to go. Finally, fearing drowning, I forced myself to swallow. My body shuddered uncontrollably as the horrible white nectar invaded my esophagus and launched its attack on my stomach. The expression on my face, combined with body tremors and a very impolite belch, gained the unwelcome attention of Alton and our host. They jabbered back and forth with obvious concern as I tried to regain my composure.

"Dear Lord," I prayed, "don't let it end like this. Please deliver me from this fate. It's worse than death. Please make whatever is in that bowl go away."

As I stared blankly at the remaining white liquid in my bowl, my life passed before my eyes. I was desperately trying to remember any sins for which I might have failed to repent, when Alton asked, "How do you like Airag?"

Yes, I was a guest in a foreign country. I was taught to be polite when I was a guest in someone else's home and to eat everything on the plate that was offered to me. I remembered the familiar cliché so often quoted by world travelers: "When in Rome, do as the Romans do."

With all of that in mind, I leaned toward Alton and said, "If I drink this stuff, I'm dead meat! Tell our host that I have a weak stomach, or whatever you have to tell him, but make it clear that I have had all the Airag I'm ever gonna have."

The look in my eyes told Alton that this was not a matter for compromise, so he turned to the host and his wife, who were staring at me with deep concern, and explained that because of my weak stomach I could not drink any more Airag. Relief spread across the faces of Mr. and Mrs. Rural Mongolia. They must have been thinking I didn't like the stuff. The jovial atmosphere returned to the yurt as Alton and our host filled their bowls again and tilted them back. I watched in total amazement. These guys were either the toughest hombres I'd ever seen or their taste buds were totally dead.

Sensing that my social blunder had not completely alienated me, I asked Alton what Airag was. He explained that it was fermented mare's milk. "Mare's milk ... you mean like horse mare's milk?" I grimaced.

"Yes," he smiled, "and it is very good to drink. It makes your skin very smooth." The only thing it did for my skin was make it crawl. I lifted the bowl to my nose and smelled it before passing it back to my host. It all made sense. It tasted like milk, with the horse still standing in it, laced with ammonia. It truly was the most revolting liquid ever to pass my lips. Gasoline smelled better than Airag and probably tasted better, too. Alton explained that in rural Mongolia, alcoholic drink was forbidden. Since the people were deprived of vodka and the like, Airag was something that they could secretly concoct ... a homebrew of sorts. But Airag was not by any means a second choice. Mongolians would prefer it to any drink.

The woman of the yurt was still concerned about my weak stomach so she asked Alton to ask me if I'd rather have some tea. Alton relayed the question and with great relief I agreed that tea would be wonderful. That was my second big mistake. I watched in horror as this little woman began to make tea. First she loaded her little one-burner stove with yak chips and started a roaring fire. There are no trees in the high Altai Mountains since the whole mountain range is well above timberline. So, the yaks furnish the firewood. All cooking and heating is done with yak chips. Next she emerged with a large metal pot filled with yet another suspicious looking white liquid and set it on top of her yak chip range.

With fear and trembling, I asked Alton what was in the pot.

"Yak milk," he replied. "It's also very good for you."

At this point I felt as if I were in some strange torture chamber. Perhaps I was going to be the first man in the world to die of Mongolian hospitality. My hostess added half a handful of rock salt to the now simmering yak milk. Then she rummaged around until she found a small black object the size and shape of a pack of cigarettes. It looked to me like a plug of chewing tobacco. It was actually a cube of compressed, dried tea leaves. She beat on one end of the cube with a small hammer until several little pieces broke off, which she added to the boiling yak milk. The addition of the small tea particles turned the boiling yak milk gray.

When the brew had come to a full boil, my stomach was already wrenching. The boulder field ... my beautiful boulder field … was looking better. The deep gripping tangle of my entire lower tract had completely surpassed the pain in my feet and legs. I yearned for a happy death plunge into a crevice between some friendly boulders. But no! I was going to endure a slow, agonizing demise as the guest of these friendly Mongolians. I could just see the newscast on TV back home: "An American hunter was found floating face down in his yak milk tea in the Altai Mountains of western Mongolia."

Finally, the tea was ready. The woman filled yet another drinking bowl, which I knew was destined for me. But before she gave it to me she added one last culinary touch: a large blob of raw yellow yak butter. It promptly melted, forming a yellow oil slick on top. Ah, now it was perfect. With the kindly expression of a mother ministering to a sick child, she handed the bowl to me. All eyes were on me as I held the bowl in trembling hands. "Dear Lord," I prayed again, "Please don't let this yak tea kill me. And Lord, please don't let it taste as bad as Airag. Amen."

Mustering all the courage left in my being, I lifted the bowl toward my mouth. Suddenly I saw myself as a World War II Japanese kamikaze pilot, knocking back his ceremonial sake before flying his plane down the smokestack of an enemy battleship. The essence of simmering yak filled my senses and sent tremors through my body once more as the bowl arrived at my lips. Perhaps it was only in my imagination, but I thought I heard a drum roll as my lips parted and the first swallow oozed out from under the oil slick. Next I saw myself standing on the gallows with the hangman's noose fit snugly around my neck. Then I imagined standing before a firing squad. Then I was being burned at the stake. I was wonderful. There was no yak tea in any of those scenes. But I couldn't postpone the inevitable any longer. Even as I tried in desperation to delay the response of my taste buds, the impulse I feared arrived at my brain, which in turn sent the devastating message to my tongue: "YUCKOOOOO! This stuff is killer yucky! Yak milk tea will knock a buzzard off a gut wagon! BARFO! Hang on to your stomach! Stand by for mega-puke!"

While still assimilating and computing all the reactionary impulses, all eyes were on me. I felt like the object of some cruel scientific experiment ... the white mouse of the Altai. As I fought for control of my convulsing body so as not to further offend my hosts, it occurred to me that barfing all over the folks might not be socially acceptable. If I struck out on yak tea, what might be next? I didn't want to know. I locked my jaws together so that nothing could escape and forced myself to swallow, in spite of the impending stomach mutiny. The mad Mongolian scientists expected me to self-destruct at any moment. With an audible gulp, the yak tea cleared my throat. Looking straight into Alton's searching eyes, I took a deep breath and said, "Great stuff!"

With applause and choruses of glee, he reported my delight to our hosts. They were obviously delighted. We were all cheering and rejoicing – they had pleased their guest and I was still alive. Alton and our host continued to drain bowls of Airag, and I sipped gingerly on my bowl of yak tea, careful not to finish it too soon and risk being offered more. Yak tea is truly repulsive. I don't think a yak could even stand it. However, yak tea would have been the worst thing I ever tasted, had I not experienced Airag first.

I always wondered why the ancient Chinese were so afraid of Genghis Kahn. Wasn't it because of his merciless tactics in battle? No, now I know the truth. The Chinese knew that if Kahn conquered China, their national drink would become Airag. That explains why they fell on their swords at the mention of his name. As I neared the bottom of my bowl of yak milk tea, I found myself looking around the yurt for a sword that I might use to prevent having to accept a second serving. It was non-alcoholic, but nonetheless it was well worth dying to avoid.

In the distance I heard the putter of the little four-cylinder Russian-made jeep. I offered up a silent prayer of thanks. I was delivered.

CHAPTER 10

Rolling For Stones

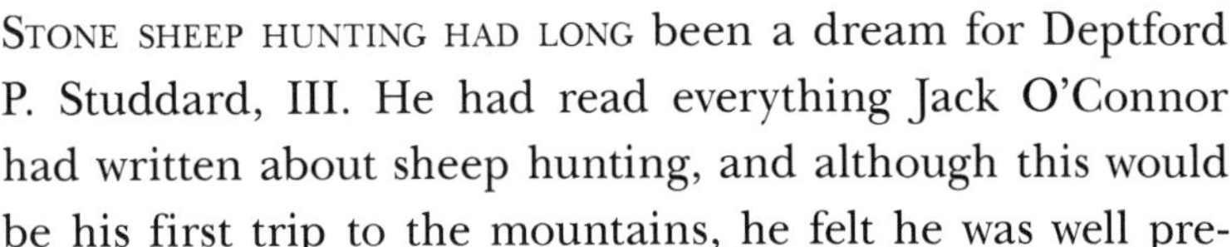

STONE SHEEP HUNTING HAD LONG been a dream for Deptford P. Studdard, III. He had read everything Jack O'Connor had written about sheep hunting, and although this would be his first trip to the mountains, he felt he was well prepared. Business had prospered and now he was going to reward himself with that hunt of a lifetime.

As he sat in his den fondling his shiny new .300 Weatherby, he felt a surge of excitement flowing through all 352 pounds of his 5'7" frame. Only a few days until he'd leave the muggy coast of Louisiana for the majestic mountains of the central Yukon. Deptford was finally going to follow O'Connor's footsteps and add his name to that elite roster of rugged mountain sheep hunters. His spirit would at last be knit with other true adventurers like Daniel Boone, Davy Crockett, and Teddy Roosevelt. Yes, there among those gallant names would be Deptford P. Studdard, III.

Deptford had waited this long for his dream hunt in part because he didn't feel that he could climb the steep stone sheep mountains on foot. But he had found an outfitter that assured him they could ride their horses right into prime sheep territory. Deptford, being a bit more gravity-bound than most, felt that this was his best bet.

On Sept. 1, 1988, Deptford first set foot on Yukon soil. His outfitter met him at the Whitehorse airport, took him to get his sheep license and chartered the floatplane.

Once in base camp, Deptford met his guide, Obie Langstrum. "Hi, I'm Deptford Studdard The Third," he said, extending his hand toward Obie. "Sure great to be here in the Yukon."

Obie lifted his nose high enough to peer out at Deptford from beneath the brim of his dilapidated black cowboy hat. "Yup," drawled Obie, spitting tobacco between Deptford's boots.

Obie was obviously one of those quiet, no-nonsense cowboys that make a mountain hunt such an interesting experience. Most of his front teeth were missing, which exposed a golf ball-sized wad of chewing tobacco every time he opened his mouth. Fortunately that wasn't very often.

Deptford was comforted to know that while Obie was not necessarily an engaging conversationalist, he was bush-wise and knew the mountains like the back of his hand. Rumor had it that if you got Obie for a guide, and if he liked you, you'd get your stone sheep. At least one of those things was already established. The rest was just a matter of time. Deptford was a real people person, and he was confident that he and Obie would be the best of buddies.

The next morning Obie appeared at the flap of Deptford's tent before dawn and explained their game plan. "Be ready to ride in ten minutes."

Deptford rolled out, stuffing his hunting gear into duffel bags. Ten minutes later, as promised, Obie appeared on horseback in front of his tent, leading Deptford's saddle horse and four packhorses. Deptford still had sleep in his eyes. Immediately Obie started stuffing bags into panniers and lashing hunting gear onto saddle pack frames. Deptford was amazed at how Obie knew exactly where every item had to go. It was intriguing to watch him mentally weigh and balance every item carefully and cinch them into place. Then finally he covered the packs with canvas and finished the job with perfect diamond hitches.

"Gee, it's amazing how well you tie all that stuff on the horses," Deptford praised.

"Hmmph," Obie grunted, "didja leave anything at home?"

Deptford was excited to see such a professional in action, but his enthusiasm waned when he saw his steed. The huge Clydesdale's belly was about chin high on Deptford, who was not a man of long stride. In fact, his legs were unusually short. The stirrups were well above his belt buckle. The good news was that Obie had definitely picked a horse that could handle Deptford's weight, which was substantially over payload for the average stone sheep hunter. The bad news was going to be getting Deptford into the saddle.

Obie grabbed his saddle horn and slithered into his saddle in one fluid motion. Deptford was impressed. "Climb on and let's ride," Obie mumbled as he stuffed half a bag of Red Man into his cheek.

Deptford stared at the stirrups, wondering how he would ever reach them. "Guess I'm gonna need a little help," he finally said with some embarrassment. Obie slung himself out of the saddle, walked over to Deptford's horse, bent over and interlocked the fingers on both hands, creating a lift up for Deptford's left foot. "What's this horse's name?" Deptford inquired as he stepped into Obie's hands.

"Name's Pete," Obie grunted, as Deptford thrust himself upward. Unfortunately, instead of gaining the required altitude, Deptford drove Obie to the ground, pinning both of the cowboy's hands under his left foot.

Obie squalled in agony. Deptford was horrified by his offence and tried to raise his left foot to free Obie before his balance was fully settled. The result only made a bad situation worse. He fell over backwards, pinning Obie for the mandatory three-count before he could wallow his way free of the irate cowboy.

Obie was coughing and gagging as if he was dying. Deptford sat speechless on the ground, wondering if he'd just killed his guide. Eventually Obie caught enough breath to cuss Deptford up one side and down the other. Besides being crushed, Obie had swallowed his plug of Red Man.

It was a bad start. Deptford could see that his hopes for establishing a pleasant relationship with Obie were dwindling. He had already alienated him and they weren't even out of base camp. In fact, Deptford had yet to reach his saddle.

Obie grabbed Pete's reins and led him over to the butt of a tree stump. "Climb up on this 'ere stump," he commanded, "and see if you can reach yer stirrups."

Deptford did as ordered, and it appeared that this would give him the extra height he needed. He stretched his left leg as high as he could and slid his boot into the stirrup. Then, with both hands on the saddle horn, he heaved himself upward once more.

But something wasn't right. The world spun before Deptford's eyes and the next thing he knew he was flat on his back, staring up at Pete's belly, where his empty saddle was now located.

Obie was now ranting and raving in his mother tongue, which afforded him some superlatives not attainable in English. Deptford crawled sheepishly out from under his tolerant steed while Obie righted and re-cinched the saddle. When the task was finished, Obie marched right up nose-to-nose with Deptford, and asked, "Whaddaya reckon ya weigh gutted?"

Deptford was taken aback. He'd never really thought about it. "Gutted? Why gutted?"

"I'm just wonderin' ... if you croak on me out here, if I can getcha back outta these hills in one piece, or if I'll have to quarter you first," Obie sneered. Deptford was stung. This Obie was one tacky cowboy. What had started as a dream hunt was quickly becoming a nightmare.

Obie led the Clydesdale back to the stump and waited in silence for the remount. Deptford dusted himself off and climbed back up on the stump. Propelled half by anger and half by fear, he thrust himself skyward once more, and to his utter delight, found himself perched astraddle his horse. Neither foot reached the stirrups, but at least he was in the saddle. Obie handed him the reins and instructed him to hold them fairly tight, allowing no droop or slack.

At last the hunt was underway. Obie took the lead, the packhorses fell into well-rehearsed ranks, and Deptford brought up the rear. Even if it had been a rocky beginning, Deptford could not help but thrill to the sight of the pack string winding ahead of him through the blazing crimson Arctic birch. The ragged sawtooth mountains, snowcapped against an azure blue morning sky, held the promise born in the heart of every sheep hunter. At last Deptford was on his way, in search of the majestic stone sheep.

Even the splendor of the scenery couldn't comfort the aching in Deptford's backside after six hours of non-stop riding. He thought Obie would stop for lunch, but that was not the case. Obie pushed ever higher into the mountains. Now every step Pete took jarred Deptford's spine like a jackhammer. His hips burned in agony; his butt felt like it was made of stone. His spine felt fused from his hips to his skull, and his head ached so intensely that he could feel his pulse in the roots of his teeth. Surely Obie would stop the death march soon ... or Deptford felt he would in fact die.

Nine hours into the ride, still without a stop, Deptford was totally numb. He buried his chin in his chest and closed his eyes, trying to think of something pleasant ... anything pleasant. He remembered that case of poison ivy that left his eyes and ears swollen shut and his festering, oozing body aflame. And there was that time the dentist slipped with the drill while performing a root canal. Who would have believed that such memories would one day be thought of as the "good old days?"

Deptford was slumped forward in a pain-induced trance when calamity struck. He had inadvertently dropped the reins, and unbeknownst to him, his Clydesdale stepped through the right rein with a big pie plate-sized hoof. This spooked the big gelding and he balked suddenly, jarring Deptford back to consciousness. He opened his eyes just in time to see himself being hurled into space as the big horse panicked and bucked for all he was worth. Deptford's life flashed before his eyes as gravity did its work.

To add the ultimate insult to injury, Obie shrieked, "I told you to hold a tight rein on that ...."

A great roaring gust of wind cut Obie off mid-sentence. It was the same wind that was leaving Deptford's lungs as he landed flat on his back. The world suddenly went dim for Deptford, who was quite certain he'd drawn his last breath.

In the meantime, Pete was pitching a wall-eyed hissy fit. Packhorses scattered like spooked quail, and Obie dismounted and ran like a wild man trying to get Pete under control. From Deptford's point of view, it was all very entertaining ... something that few men get to see just before they die. He felt strangely detached from the mayhem. An eerie peace settled over him. He'd never thought much about dying. "The mountains would be a nice place to die," he thought. "My grandchildren will hear stories about their grandpa, who died on the hunt, just like all those other famous mountain men. I'll be sort of a family legend. It's pretty and quiet here in the land of the eagle, the sheep and the bear ... and Obie! Not Obie! Oh God! If I die here, he'll bring me back quartered up like a moose! I'll be disgraced forever!"

Deptford's breath returned and with it the reality of the rodeo still in progress.

As Obie grabbed Pete's reins, the big horse reared down firmly on his left ankle. The resounding snap echoed like a rifle shot across the valley. Suddenly, with superhuman strength, supercharged by immeasurable pain, Obie yanked the huge beast to a nearby tree and tied his head up so tight that he had bark in both nostrils.

Deptford was amazed at Obie's feat of strength. Then Obie turned toward him, and for the first time since his ankle snapped, Deptford could see the rage in Obie's eyes. Before he could speak, Obie had him by collar and he was shaking him like a dishrag. "I told you to keep them reins high, you tinhorn tub-o-guts!" Obie screamed. "If you ever drop yer reins again, I'll kill ya! Ya understand?"

With that, Obie dropped Deptford back to the ground in a heap. Then he turned and hobbled off toward the tangled wreckage of horses, pack saddles and panniers, which were strewn about the balsam trees.

Deptford, a quick learner, felt sure he would require no further instruction on how high to hold the reins. But how many more lessons were there to learn about sheep hunting? He wasn't sure how many more his body could endure.

Eventually the feeling returned to Deptford's backside. He grabbed a small balsam tree and pulled himself to a standing position. After several minutes of experimental teetering in one spot, he took his first step. His legs seemed disconnected from his brain. All the concentration he could muster would not direct his feet where he wanted them to go. They just flopped along, landing in the most unexpected places. How would those legs ever stalk a stone sheep? How would they climb back into the saddle? For the first time, Deptford felt imprisoned ... trapped in his folly. He had to face facts. Maybe he wasn't stone sheep hunting material after all. At best he was suited for bear bait. He had to embrace the fact that he wasn't having much fun.

As Deptford did a mental inventory of his physical agony, he realized how dreadfully hungry he was. Obie had started a fire and seemed to be organizing the camp for the night. Deptford took a deep breath and hobbled sorely toward the fire. "What's for dinner?" he asked politely. Obie's silent sociopathic glare pierced the darkness and made the hair on the back of Deptford's neck stand on end. A shiver raced up his spine. He suddenly felt like a man who had come to supper, only to find that he was the main course. All he wanted was something to eat after nearly 12 hours on the trail.

Obie rummaged through the panniers. "Here you go," he said, as he pitched Deptford a large Spanish onion. "Looks like you could stand to lose a pound or two."

Deptford snatched the onion out of the air like a shortstop fielding a line drive. He stared blankly at it for a moment, stunned at the thought of dining on a solitary onion.

"Is this it?" he asked faintly.

"Naw, we'll have some coffee soon as the water boils," Obie replied.

Deptford sat down on a log, warming his aching body by the fire. And there in solemn darkness, he ate the onion.

The next morning Deptford was shocked from his sleep by Obie violently shaking him. "Oh no," Deptford thought. "He's come back for the kill!"

"Get up quick!" Obie hissed. "There's a band of rams right above camp. If you hurry you'll have a ram before lunch!"

Suddenly Deptford's fear turned to excitement. He'd almost forgotten why he'd come. But Obie's words recharged his desire to bag a stone sheep. His adrenaline surged and he leapt from his sleeping bag in spite of the pain. As he stumbled out of the tent, still tying his boots laces, he saw Obie sitting on the ground with one eye jammed into the lens of his spotting scope. "There's nine rams," Obie said calmly, "and one of 'em will go close to 40 inches."

"Forty inches," Deptford gasped. "How do we get him?"

"We'll have to sneak up that little draw to that patch of timber. Then we'll sneak downhill 'til we can see 'em there where they're feeding," Obie explained. "You ready to go?"

Deptford grabbed his Weatherby and stuffed four fat .300 Magnum cartridges into the magazine. "Yeah, I'm ready!" he snapped.

Obie flowed over the broken terrain like water, and Deptford limped along. They covered the quarter mile to the bottom of the draw in minutes. Then they climbed up the draw to the stand of stunted balsams as planned. Obie turned to a gasping Deptford and said, "We'll stop here long enough for you to catch yer breath and calm down ... then when yer ready, we'll slip down through the trees 'til we can see 'em. You'll have to get steady and make yer shot before they spook."

Deptford gasped and nodded.

After the short rest, Obie led Deptford cautiously down through the timber, stopping every two or three steps and straining to catch sight of the rams. "There they are," Obie whispered, stopping mid-step. "Lay down and get a good rest, and I'll tell you which ram to shoot."

Deptford did as instructed. He snuggled in behind a log and rested his Weatherby.

"It's the ram at the far left, above the red rock," Obie whispered. "Just get real steady before you shoot."

Fifteen seconds passed. "You got him in your scope?"

"No," Deptford whispered back, "I can't see him."

"He's the one on the far left, above that red rock," Obie repeated. "Can you see him now?"

"No, I can't see him," Deptford gasped. "I can't see anything!"

"Whaddaya mean, you can't see anything?" Obie snapped.

"I mean I can't see anything!" Deptford hissed. "Everything is black through this scope ... I can't see anything but black!"

At that point the big rams vanished like a puff of smoke. It was over.

Obie snatched the rifle out of Deptford's hands and looked through the scope. "I can see just fine through this scope," he screamed. "What's a matter with you? Stand up here and look through this scope and tell me what you see!"

"I still can't see a thing," Deptford cringed.

"Well, it's no stinkin' wonder!" Obie sputtered. "The stock's four inches too long for ya. Ain'tcha ever shot this gun before?"

Deptford hadn't. He'd bought the rifle just for this hunt and a local gunsmith had sighted it in for him. Until this moment, he had no idea that the stock was too long.

Obie yanked the rifle out of Deptford's hands and headed down the draw, kicking up little puffs of dust with each long, aggravated step. He reverted once again to his mother tongue. When Deptford arrived at camp, to his horror, there was Obie, bent over his brand new Weatherby with a Swede saw, halfway through the butt of the fancy, mirror-finished walnut. Deptford stood in bewildered silence, afraid to speak, as Obie finished the job. The butt of the beautiful stock fell to the ground, and Obie turned to Deptford and thrust the rifle into his hands. "Now look through the scope!" he commanded. Deptford did. "Can ya see now?"

To Deptford's amazement, the coarse circumcision of his fancy walnut stock had done the trick. He could see. "Perfect," Deptford replied.

"Well, that dumb stunt cost you a 40-incher," Obie growled. "Ya don't get a chance at a sheep like that every day."

If feeling bad was of any consequence, Deptford's debt was paid in full.

The next morning the pack train continued deeper into the mountains. Obie took the lead as usual and rode without stopping. Deptford mentally prepared for another day of equestrian agony and bit the bullet as the various parts of his lower anatomy were systematically altered from burning pain to aching numbness. At 3 p.m. Obie stopped the procession unexpectedly and dismounted. Deptford, now completely numb from the waist down, and desperate for relief, leaned hard to the starboard until he toppled from the saddle, landing with a resounding whump. Obie tied up the horses while Deptford massaged his knees.

Long before Deptford could stand, Obie set up his spotting scope and began glassing for sheep. Deptford asked, "Is this a good sheep area?"

"Yup, sometimes," Obie elaborated.

They were on a high mountain plateau, which broke away before them in several huge descending terraced steps. The vista was breathtaking. At the bottom of the grass-covered terrace the mountain dropped off into a sheer, steep valley with nothing but eagle pasture for a thousand feet below. At the bottom, like a thin silver ribbon, a river followed its serpentine course out of the high country. The awesome beauty of it all made Deptford temporarily forget his pain.

'There's a band of rams," Obie whispered. "Down at the lip of that second bench below us, right where the grassy part of the bench meets them big boulders."

Deptford raised his binoculars and saw the salt and pepper-colored dots that Obie was talking about, but they were too far to judge with binoculars. "Any good ones in the bunch?" Deptford inquired.

"There's a couple that'll do," Obie replied. "They're bedded down, but they'll be getting up to feed within an hour, so we'll have to put a move on 'em right quick. Are ya ready to go?"

Deptford looked down at his failing legs. "I'm not sure."

"What now?" Obie challenged.

"Well, er, I'm not sure I can walk yet," Deptford offered sheepishly.

"Stand up!" Obie commanded.

Deptford tried but his legs would not cooperate. They were still so numb he could hardly feel them.

"Well, ain't this a fine howdy-do," came Obie's rant. "Here I am, out in the middle of these here mountains, huntin' stone sheep with a man that can't even stand up on his own hind legs.

"Tell me this, Mr. Stone Sheep Hunter, did you think I was gonna carry your oversized carcass down there to those sheep? Well, if you did, you're dead wrong!"

Deptford was under the gun and he knew it. If he botched another attempt at a sheep, he was sure that Obie would give up on him. His mind was racing, trying to figure out a way to move himself before Obie came completely unglued. His legs were out of the question. But at least it was downhill to the sheep.

"What about it, Spider Man?" Obie jabbed. "We gonna sit here and wish them sheep to death, or we gonna go down there and shoot one? This here's the last place I know of where we're gonna find sheep below us. If you can't haul yer butt downhill, you sure as heck ain't gonna out-climb one. This is yer last chance ... what's it gonna be?"

"Yes," thought Deptford, "it is downhill ... if nothing else, gravity is on my side."

If necessity was indeed the mother of invention, Deptford was about to give birth to one of the most innovative sheep stalks in the history of hunting.

"I can do it!" Deptford shouted.

"You can?" Obie asked suspiciously.

"Yes, I can get down there ... I know I can," Deptford said with a determined gleam in his eye. "I can't stand up or walk down there, but I can roll down off this bench. I'll just point myself in the right direction and roll as far as I need to go!"

Obie was dumbfounded. "Yer gunna roll down this mountain?"

"Why not?" Deptford argued. "I came here to get a stone sheep and I'm not goin' home without one."

Obie scratched his head, raised one eyebrow thoughtfully and spit a stream of tobacco. "Dangdest thing I ever heard of," he mumbled.

"Well, whaddaya say?" Deptford asked with increasing courage.

"Might work," Obie said cautiously.

Deptford was inspired; his faith in the hunt was renewed. For the first time since it all began, he felt he was truly in control. "Obie, you carry my rifle and my binoculars," he commanded. "I'll start off the side of this bench and you just stay close and tell me which way to roll. Then, when we get to where we want to be, just hand me my rifle and tell me which sheep is the biggest, and I'll make you proud. Deptford P. Studdard The Third didn't come all the way to the Yukon to be outsmarted by a sheep!"

Obie was impressed by Deptford's newfound confidence. It was bizarre, but they were going after the sheep.

"Here I go," Deptford announced as he held his arms at his side, lay down on his back and flung himself over the edge of the plateau. Obie was at his side as Deptford launched his unique descent. One roll ... two rolls ... three rolls, and down the grassy bench he went.

"Nothing to this!" Deptford cried victoriously.

"Yer doin' good!" Obie said, offering his first words of encouragement since the hunt began.

Deptford was picking up a little speed. His body flopped along with a rhythmic cadence: kerblump ... kerblump ... kerblump. Obie picked up his pace from a stroll to a slow trot.

"Yer makin' good time now," Obie cheered as Deptford picked up still more momentum.

"I think I'm gettin' outta control," Deptford gasped.

"Then stop a minute," Obie yelled.

"I caaaaan't!" Deptford moaned as his kerblump ... kerblump increased to a steady rumbling bump-a-da-bump-ad-a-bump-a-da-bump.

Deptford was in serious trouble. Suddenly he shot downhill in a blur. Obie was running as hard as he could, but Deptford was pulling away.

"Wait for me," screamed Obie as he slung Deptford's rifle over his shoulder. Obie was running on one sprained ankle, which did nothing for his speed. Deptford was a bouncing blur, racing downward, completely out of control. He looked like an overgrown whirligig, his arms flapping like undersized propellers. Another 50 yards and he would break over the top of the second bench. If that happened before he could get himself under control, there would be no stopping him. He'd roll right through the middle of the rams like a gargantuan bowling ball, and then shoot out into space for at least a thousand feet before he landed in the rocks in creek bottom below. Deptford was on a suicide mission, now only 40 yards from the next bench.

"If ya don't kill yerself, I'll do it for ya!" Obie screamed as he shifted down for more speed. He was now within five yards of the human rollerball. Now only three yards separated the two men in their death race. With all the grace of an Olympic diver, Obie vaulted forward, landing on top of Deptford. In a great cloud of dirt and rolling stones, Obie bulldogged Deptford to a grinding halt, just before he was about to cross the brink of no return. When the dust settled, Obie was sprawled over the huge belly of the battered Cajun.

"Is this the right spot?" asked Deptford with amazing clarity.

Obie had forgotten all about the rams. He looked up, and to his amazement all the rams were standing 150 yards below, staring up at the two men. The rams had obviously never seen such a spectacle and were not sure what they'd just witnessed.

"Yeah! The rams are right under us!" Obie whispered. "Here, roll over and shoot the one with the black cape!" he said as he peeled the rifle off his back, chambered a round and stuffed it into Deptford's shoulder.

Deptford took a rest on his elbows, centered the crosshairs on the big ram's chest and pulled the trigger. When he did, the recoil jammed the scope back into his eye, cutting a perfect half moon over his right eye.

"Ya got 'em!" screamed Obie. "Ya gotcherself a stone sheep!"

Deptford managed to rise up on his elbows before shock overcame him. Obie turned and saw Deptford's good eye roll back in his head. The other eye was full of blood from the cut over his eye. "I got 'em," Deptford gasped and passed out cold.

It was nearly 20 minutes before Deptford came to. He was sprung, bruised and battered. Obie, knowing that his hunter was in serious trouble, built a fire, covered him with blankets, left food and water, and rode like the wind back to base camp. He covered the 25 miles in record time and radioed Whitehorse for a helicopter evacuation.

Deptford spent a week in the hospital, nursing broken ribs, bruises and contusions.

Today, when Deptford gazes at the beautiful stone sheep mount hanging over his mantle, he recalls the majesty of the Yukon, the grandeur of the mountains, and the thrill of the hunt. He remembers his crusty mountain guide, the onion he ate for supper, and the nonstop equestrian death marches that almost left him paralyzed from the waist down. He remembers how he overcame adversity when his legs failed him, how he rolled to the brink of death, and made the shot of his life.

And he remembers that case of poison ivy that left his body aflame, and that time the dentist slipped with the drill while performing a root canal. Who would have believed that such memories would one day be considered the good old days?

CHAPTER 11

Black Day on the Brazos

ACCORDING TO ALL WHO KNEW him before that dark day, Brother Dudley's word was as good as gold. He was a straight shooter – a man of great integrity. Even today, some still feel that way about him. Had it not been for his one great weakness, there probably would never have been a reason to doubt the man. No chink in his armor, no shadow of suspicion cast.

But turkey hunting will eventually tell on a man. It has a way of bringing deeply buried things to the surface.

I make no judgment in Brother Dudley's case, although certain facts challenge one's best efforts to remain objective. I will present his story and let you judge for yourself. If I could offer anything of a personal bias, it would be to encourage the reader to consider what you are about to read in light of

Brother Dudley's exemplary life as a devoted husband, father and minister of the Gospel. To my knowledge he has no criminal record and has never been convicted of a felony.

Date: April 14, 1992
Place: Shackleford County, Texas
Time: Daybreak

Brother Dudley sat huddled hopefully in an ancient pecan bottom, waiting for dawn to break above the banks of the Brazos River. In another location, 200 yards away, Shallow Jack Deere, his friend and turkey-hunting partner, also sat in darkness. (Shallow Jack Deere is also known to be a man of honor. He is a seminary graduate and devoted Bible scholar. Prior to this event, he had never been known to be part to any shady or skullduggerous schemes or practices.)

Brother Dudley was clad from head to toe in the appropriate camouflage and was armed with a small caliber rifle and a devastating new turkey call. This new call was so deadly that it was rumored to have been banned in several Southern states. Rather than imitating the language of love of the female turkey, this call duplicated the voices of two irate gobblers engaged in battle. While girl talk would fool a gobbler every now and then, the sound of two gobblers fighting was more than any red-blooded tom could resist. Brother Dudley was determined to dupe some West Texas turkeys with it before it was completely outlawed.

As darkness gradually retreated, a barred owl announced the coming day, and in the distance a gobbler responded aggressively from his roost. This was the signal Brother Dudley was waiting to hear.

With a call in each hand, Brother Dudley began pumping the plungers with his thumbs, creating the chortles and purrs that gobblers make in combat. After a minute or two he stopped and listened for a response, but all was silent.

Brother Dudley soon resumed his fighting purrs. In spite of the eerie stillness, he was confident of success. Turkeys were his forte. He spoke their language well. It was just a matter of time.

After 20 minutes of sporadic calling, Brother Dudley saw movement in the timber. He slowly laid his calls on the ground beside him and wrapped his hands around the stock of his .22-250. In an instant four gobblers walked boldly out of the timber 150 yards in front of him. They were not tiptoeing suspiciously in single file as gobblers typically do when they come to the call. Not these birds. They looked like the James gang, walking defiantly into Dodge, four abreast, hands above their holsters, just itching for a good fight.

Though somewhat amazed at the brazen audacity of the incoming gobblers, Brother Dudley knew that a turkey in the field was as good as in the pan. All he had to do was sit perfectly still and wait. And come they did. At an estimated

60 yards, the gobblers stopped to look for the fight they believed they were about to find. Brother Dudley centered his crosshairs on the largest of the four and touched the trigger. At the sound of the shot his gobbler hit the ground with a thud. The deed was done. Brother Dudley had once again outsmarted the wariest of all game birds.

But something was different this time. Instead of streaking for cover, the other three turkeys stood their ground. These were determined birds, to say the least. Brother Dudley could easily have shot another, but since the remaining three were showing no signs of fear he thought he might be able to sneak back through the timber and bring Shallow Jack up for a crack at them. In spite of the shot and their fallen comrade, the turkeys stood their ground, obviously still intent on locating the fighting toms they had come to see.

Brother Dudley leaned his rifle against a tree and was slinking back into the timber toward Shallow Jack when he thought he saw his dead turkey move. So, he stopped to get a better look. Sure enough, there were some signs of life. It seemed his dead turkey was not so dead after all. At first the shot seemed perfect, but obviously it hadn't done the job completely. Twitches turned to flops and soon the turkey was far too lively to leave alone. Brother Dudley was now unarmed, so he'd have to grab a stick or a limb to use as a club to finish off the turkey.

However, the closer he came to the turkey, the more he tried to get away. Brother Dudley could see that the turkey was flopping his way toward the riverbank, so he made a dash for the crippled bird. But the turkey was too fast. He flopped over the steep bank and toppled down to the landing at the water's edge 12 feet below.

Now Brother Dudley and the turkey both faced a crisis. Brother Dudley couldn't follow the turkey down the straight drop-off, and the turkey had to decide how to handle being trapped between Brother Dudley and the river.

The gobbler looked up at Brother Dudley and then turned his head and stared contemplatively at the river. The wheels were turning and a decision was at hand. Finally, the turkey made a desperate move – one that no turkey hunter but Brother Dudley had ever witnessed. He flung himself squarely into the Brazos River.

A turkey wasn't made for water, and it was an ungainly spectacle to see the big bird spraddled awkwardly in the flowing water. Caught in the current, the courageous bird started to drift downstream. Brother Dudley meanwhile had decided his best option was to go back for his rifle, return, put the turkey out of his misery, and then fish him out of the river farther downstream. The plan made sense at the time.

Shallow Jack had heard the shot and walked up to Brother Dudley just as he was about to abandon the turkey to retrieve his rifle. It was at that point that Brother Dudley claims to have pointed out his floating turkey to Shallow Jack. Shallow Jack agrees that he was, in fact, a witness to the gobbler adrift in the river.

Then a bizarre thing happened. From the depths of the Brazos, a huge fish savagely attacked the floating turkey, grabbing the bird in its cavernous jaws and pulling him under the surface to a watery grave. Brother Dudley and Shallow Jack both report watching the huge fish writhing and rolling in the deep water, as it swallowed the ill-fated gobbler whole. Then, as suddenly as it began, the water ceased to boil, leaving only a muddy cloud as a grim reminder of how tough a turkey's life can be.

As the story of the great turkey-eating fish circulated throughout the South, two questions emerged. First, what kind of fish could possibly be big enough to swallow a full-grown turkey? Fishermen who know the Brazos well believe it had to have been a huge flathead catfish. Flatheads in excess of 100 pounds have been caught in the Brazos. Other fishermen ventured the possibility of a huge alligator gar, or even an alligator, although no one can recall any alligators in the upper Brazos in recent times.

Turkey hunters, on the other hand, did not immediately embrace the possibility of a turkey-eating fish and were more inclined to ask: "How dumb does Brother Dudley think we really are?"

Admittedly, some grace was lacking in their response. One longtime turkey hunter commented, "It ain't no crime to come home without no turkey. It happened to me once. I just missed him, that's all!"

It has been said that the truth can't be found in any turkey hunter.

Interviews with wives and children of devoted turkey hunters offer yet another possibility – that turkey hunters in general lack the ability to discern facts from fiction. One anonymous turkey hunter's wife said of her former husband, "By the end of the turkey season that man couldn't tell ya his name. He'd walk around here in a daze, with a glazed look in his eyes. Kinda reminded me of one of them serial killers. Nothin' he mighta said in turkey season would'a surprised me one bit!"

In conclusion, it appears that turkey hunting should probably be viewed as an affliction. There is substantial evidence to support the popular belief that a long season of continuous turkey hunting renders the turkey hunter incapable of differentiating the real from the imaginary. Apparently they blend together so well in his mind that he perceives everything as real.

Those who know and love Brother Dudley will stand by him and see him through the humiliation of this incident. To them it doesn't matter what happened to his turkey. But Brother Dudley is still sticking to his incredible story, just the way he believes he remembers it. Strangely, though, he seems to have lost his interest in turkey hunting. Rumor has it that he's spending his spare time fishing these days out on the Brazos in Shackleford County.

CHAPTER 12

Titty Brim and My Near Death Experience

AFTER HEARING GRANDIOSE TALES OF Johnny Tanner's private lake, I finally ended up fishing it with my old friend Richard Culpepper. Richard had promised me that if I ever got to Carrolton, Ga., he would take me to Johnny's lake. It supposedly was filled with giant Titty Brim and largemouth bass. The day finally came when Johnny, Richard and I were at the lake of my dreams.

Richard was shamelessly fishing off the dock with a fish food pellet wedged into the bend of a small brim book while Johnny and I boarded a small boat so I could fly fish for bass. Suddenly I began to feel strange. In fact, it felt like the telltale signs of a heart attack. My dream fishing was turning into a nightmare. I told Johnny I was pretty sure I was having a heart attack. He immediately pointed the boat back to the dock where Richard was still dipping his fish food pellet in hopes of tricking a "Titty Brim" into biting.

For the benefit of those not from the Southeast, a "Titty Brim" is a brim too large to hold in one hand, so you have to hold it against your breast with one hand while you remove your hook with the other. Johnny and I were almost to the dock when Richard landed a Titty Brim. So, as I agonized with death looming, Richard shouted, "Hey Russ, look at the size of this baby!"

I appreciated his enthusiasm, but I wasn't interested, especially since he had tricked the fish into biting with a food pellet! I suppose it could be argued that he was merely matching the hatch, but somehow it seemed like cheating.

When we made it into the house, I remembered hearing that taking aspirin was helpful when having a heart attack. Johnny found some baby aspirins and brought them downstairs. He and Richard read the instructions on the bottle, trying to figure out how many baby aspirins it took to equal one adult aspirin. I soon realized that I might be cold in my grave before they figured it out so I told them to forget the math and just give me a handful so we could head for the hospital.

It was a high-speed trip of about 15 minutes to the Tanner Medical Center in Carrolton where I was ushered into the emergency room. The doctor determined that I was having a serious atrial fibrillation issue that caused my heart rate to race to well over 260 beats per minute. Though I was not having a heart attack, had I not gotten to the hospital when I did, it would have ended in one. He gave me a shot that slowed my heart rate down and saved my bacon.

The only bed available was in the intensive care unit, so that became my new home. Once my heart rate was somewhat stabilized, I began to feel better. But I had a serious problem.

During the night the on-duty nurse figured out that I was the editor of a deer-hunting magazine and she flipped out. She was an avid deer hunter, and I was her captive audience while she told me her best deer stories, how she gutted, skinned, and butchered her own deer, and how she made her own deer jerky, which she eventually smuggled into my room for me to sample. She even went so far as to tell me of her tradition of peeing on the spot where her deer died. I was not exactly clear what prompted that tradition, but she said she was part Native American, so that might have explained it.

The first morning in the ICU I awoke to find the meal cart at my bedside. On it sat the shiny silver-domed cover that hid my breakfast. The note on top had two words in bold print: **"HEART HEALTHY."**

I wasn't sure what to expect, but I assumed the worst as I lifted the dome to see what succulent delight constituted a heart-healthy breakfast. To my utter amazement there were scrambled eggs and bacon and two giant cathead biscuits swimming in cream gravy! Naturally I gobbled it up as fast as I could in case there had been a mistake. I couldn't help but wonder what, if that were truly heart-healthy, a normal breakfast would have been.

A couple of days passed, in which time I ate lots more homemade jerky and heart-healthy meals! Then I was discharged. It was time to head home to Montgomery, Ala., where I was to seek further medical help.

Richard and some of his business associates had bought a limousine and would hire a driver to take them to the Atlanta airport when they had to fly out on business. He insisted on having his driver take me back to Montgomery in his limo. He even had one of his employees drive my car home. So, my wife Sharleen and I sat there in that huge limo for the ride home in grand style – she reading a book and me nibbling on my stash of homemade jerky. I couldn't help but think of how Jeff Foxworthy would have described what I was doing … "You might be a Redneck if you're on a road trip in a long black limo while eating homemade deer jerky."

In Montgomery the testing began to see how to control my serious "afib" problem. My doctor tried shocking my heart with the electric paddles to no avail. My heart refused to return to sinus rhythm. He explained that my problem was caused by the electrical system in my heart getting out of sync. In other words, the circuitry, which causes everything to work in proper sequence, was broken. A short in the system, if you will. I was put on medication that kept my heart rate so low that I felt like I was constantly towing the Queen Mary through an ocean of corn syrup.

The next step was to try an oblation. This procedure, if it works, is an instant cure. I had high hopes until I found that they could not reach the problem area of my heart. Back to square one.

Medication had my heart beating so slow that I was not functional enough to work or drive or even think clearly. On one of my visits to the heart doctor an officious nurse approached me and asked the dreaded question: "Mr. Thornberry, have we discussed your diet?"

Though my thinking was slow, I recognized that things were about to change for the worse. Steak and mashed potatoes flashed before my eyes and faded away into a fond memory of the good ol' days. The doctor asked me to follow her to her desk and told me to take a chair, which I did. Apparently the news was going to be too much to digest while standing.

"Mr. Thornberry, what I have to tell you is VERY important and it is imperative that you follow my guidelines exactly," she said.

I nodded in resigned despair.

"You must under no circumstances," she paused to see if I was paying attention, "eat . . . Brussels sprouts or drink green tea. Do you understand?"

I slowly processed the bad news and looked around to see if I was on Candid Camera.

She folded her arms and stared at me, awaiting my reply.

I assumed the most disappointed demeanor I could muster and said, "Okay I promise."

Then I was dismissed.

I walked away wondering how I would make it through life without Brussels sprouts and green tea, both of which I despised. I held back my laughter until I was out of her sight. That was undoubtedly the best bad news I had ever heard!

I finally asked my personal doctor if there might be a plan C or D. With a heartbeat of 30 beats per minute, I could hardly see how I was going to do much of anything. He told me that there was one surefire cure and that would be to install a pacemaker. I was thrilled and asked to get it ASAP.

When I arrived at the hospital on the day of surgery, the nurses took all my vital signs and prepped me for the operation, which included hooking me up to an IV.

Finally I was put on a gurney and wheeled into the operating room. There was no one there but me and the anesthesiologist, who introduced himself. "Hi, I'm Robert," he chirped, "I'll be your bartender and I'll make you a very happy man."

I liked his style.

Eventually they rolled me onto the operating table and tucked me in tightly under the sheets with a little box over my face so I couldn't see anything. I'm not sure if that was for my sake or theirs, but it was a little weird. When all was in place, the doctor began the procedure with an incision that nearly ripped me out of my shackles. I screamed like a banshee, which startled everyone, to say the least. They weren't expecting me to be conscious at that point. Immediately there was a scurrying all around me, while I vigorously protested the protocol. What the hell was going on?! I couldn't believe that I was supposed to be carved on while I was wide awake.

A few minutes passed and the doctor began again, and again I screamed blue murder. More shuffling, more whispering, and now searching for the IV tube, which was supposed to be carrying the elixir that Robert had promised. After some time they found that the little pinch mechanism was still on the tube, preventing the anesthesia from reaching Yours Truly. I don't remember anything from the moment they removed it.

Apart for that little mishap the surgery went perfectly and I felt like my old self almost immediately. Before being discharged from the hospital I got my marching orders, which forbade me to exert myself or lift anything over ten pounds for a number of weeks. After the prescribed weeks of leisure I could resume doing whatever I would normally do.

My non-exertion probation period ended two days before I was to take a group of men to Alaska for a bear hunt and some halibut fishing.

Our group boarded two cabin cruisers at Seward and began our 2-hour trip out to Prince of Wales Island, where we would spend the next five days. We were no sooner out of port than we were blasted by an incoming storm with fierce winds and 12-foot waves. The only thing we could do was stay pointed into the storm, which caused our trip to last five long hours. The hunters that were not seafaring sorts (most of them) chummed their guts out over the stern.

Even after the storm subsided, the weather was bitterly cold. We were hunting in torrential downpours and near freezing temperatures. We lived aboard the cabin cruisers and boarded inflatable boats to travel among the floating glacial ice formations in and out of coves along the coastline. The only two bears dumb enough to be prowling around in that weather became rugs. After the hunt, my friend Kenny Thacker stayed on with me for some halibut fishing, which definitely trumped the bear hunting. We went home with a load of fresh, frozen, vacuum-sealed halibut steaks.

As soon as I arrived home in Montgomery, I noticed that I was feeling draggy again like I did before the pacemaker surgery. At my routine checkup, I told the nurse about how I was feeling. She soon discovered that I had pulled the wire from the pacemaker out of my heart. "What have you been doing?" she inquired. "Just doing what I normally do," I replied.

So the date for wire reattachment surgery was set.

Going back to the hospital for the second surgery was truly a déjà vu experience. Again I was on my back on the gurney and being wheeled back into the operating room. Once again, it was just the anesthesiologist and me. I could scarcely believe my eyes – it was Robert!

He was going about his routine when I casually popped the question.

"Your name is Robert, isn't it?"

Surprised, he turned toward me. "Yes, do I know you?"

"Probably not," I replied, "but I remember you."

He looked confused.

"Well Robert, I'm the guy who nearly went through pacemaker surgery 'au naturale' because you forgot to take the clip off the IV."

I could almost read the words "lawsuit" expressed in his eyes, so I let him stew in his own juice for a moment before I continued.

"Not to worry, Robert," I said, "I have completely forgiven you for that little mishap. Heck, everybody makes a little boo boo now and then, but I do want you to know that if it happens again you're dead meat!"

"Oh, no sir," Robert exclaimed! "I'm giving you a double shot this time and you'll never feel a thing!"

Robert was true to his word. I woke up after surgery without the slightest unpleasant memory.

I had asked the doctor before the first surgery if she could put the pacemaker on the right side of my chest instead of the normal position of the left side. I explained that I shoot rifles and shotguns off my left shoulder, which I could not do if the pacemaker were on the left side. She said that she could accommodate my request and would simply use a longer piece of wire to span the distance from the device to my heart. Apparently the wire had been a bit short for my kind of normal life, so the second time she not only used a longer wire but she even sewed an extra loop to my heart for good measure. So no matter what I did, I couldn't come up short.

It's been eight years since then and life has returned to my kind of normal. I am once again free to eat all the Brussels sprouts and drink all the green tea I want!

CHAPTER 13

Mother Nature is a Mean Old Woman

A SUNNY JULY EVENING ON Little Chickakoo Lake west of Edmonton, Alberta, stands out in my memories of notable fly-fishing excursions. As I have often said, there is a strange little cloud that follows me when I go hunting or fishing. I'm always on guard for what the cloud might drop on me, but on this evening I thought I was home free.

The kokanee had cooperated wonderfully; the evening was a picture of blissful serenity. Rich golden light painted the lake as the sun dipped toward the horizon. The water was like a mirror of the deep blue sky. A pair of loons yodeled to one another. The evening was cooling, and I could think of nothing more pleasant than just sitting there in my canoe, soaking up the sounds and scenes.

There are rare moments in an outdoorsman's life when Mother Nature is compassionate. She is friendly, letting the soft blanket of a summer evening drape gently across your shoulders. It's almost like a peace offering after many battles. When it happens, the outdoorsman relaxes and allows himself to become vulnerable and trusting. This gift was personal and obviously just for me. I was the only fisherman on the lake. Such was that perfect July evening.

Finally, as the timber swallowed the sun and the falling temperature allowed me to see my breath, I turned the canoe toward the landing where I had parked my truck below a high bluff. I tried to paddle softly so as not to make a noise that would interrupt the harmony. At that moment I felt that nature and I truly were one.

It was surreal.

When I was about ten yards from the bank, I heard a roar above me. Stunned, I looked up just in time to see a 1976 Chevrolet soaring off the top of the bluff. Its trajectory would in fact take it nose-first into my canoe.

"Oh, this is just great," I thought. "I'll be the first man in history to get run over by a car while paddling a canoe."

I gave an instinctive, adrenaline-surged side push with my paddle that undoubtedly saved my life. The Chevy landed on its belly in the 4-foot deep water beside me with all the grace of a land mine. The impact lifted my canoe and me completely out of the water. (It's hard to think clearly when you're being run over by a car while canoeing.)

The next thing I remember was standing chest deep in Little Chickakoo with the entire lake heaving around me. And there was the priceless view of the top of a lime green Chevrolet parked where my canoe had been only a second before.

A flood of relief shot through my body as I realized I had survived. Then relief turned into unbridled anger. I wanted to get my hands fixed firmly around the throat of the idiot driver. As I approached the car I could see the dazed faces of three inebriated teenagers that looked like they'd been struck by lightning. Even in their stupor, they knew they'd screwed up in a big way.

I managed to get myself under control although I was very near the snapping point, so I thought it best to retrieve my canoe and leave before I did something I'd regret.

I righted my canoe and started pulling it toward shore, passing within a few feet of the three drunken Musketeers. As I slid the canoe past the driver's side door, the dazed kid looked at me with eyes that clearly revealed no one was home. "What are we going to do?" he asked.

I considered his question for a moment and then replied somewhat sarcastically. "WE are not going to do anything. I am going to load up MY canoe and go home. The question is, 'What are YOU going to do?' Have a great evening."

I replayed the event while driving back to Edmonton, thanking God for my good fortune. It had been quite an experience. Then my thoughts drifted back to the aforementioned cloud that I thought had forgotten me for once. WRONG!

I fell for the oldest trick in the book: believing that Mother Nature had a compassionate heart. But that simply allowed me to drop my guard before the "GOTCHA."
I could hear her laughing. In spite of all her glory that she uses to lull one into a false sense of security, Mother Nature is still a mean old woman!

Trust me.

CHAPTER 14

Summer Vacation

DURING THE SUMMER OF 1963, my two best friends, Buster Goff and Lynn Smith, and I decided to make a quick trip out to Southern California from our hometown of Corpus Christi, Texas. Since none of us had the money to go in style, we decided to make the trip in my 1960 Chevy.

We scratched up enough money for gas and perhaps a few meals. According to our naive calculations, as long as we didn't meet with any major calamities, we'd make it. Of course our shortage of funds was to be paired with survival skills like hunting and fishing along the way. Lynn's father took a dim view of the little .22 we packed in the truck, but we assured him it was perfectly safe and essential for our grocery supplement program. Our youthful confidence exceeded our collective common sense by a considerable margin. We were full of optimism when we pulled out of Corpus Christi.

The plan was to drive north to Colorado, then head west across Utah and Nevada until we reached Lake Tahoe. We would then drive south until we hit Santa Maria. My parents had stayed there when my father retired after 22 years in the Navy. After a brief visit with them, we would deadhead back across Arizona, New Mexico and then head south through the belly of the Lone Star State until we reached the Gulf Coast once again. It was terribly ambitious, but young men thrive on the brink of impossibility (and poor judgment).

Buster had a friend in Amarillo, so we drove a nonstop leg of nearly 580 miles to get there. We spent a short night at Buster's friend's place.

Dawn broke a beautiful clear, calm morning on the endless rural landscape of undulating hills and prairie grass. Just as the subject of breakfast arose, I spotted some likely candidates alongside the desolate highway. Though I'd never before seen a living chukar partridge, I recognized them immediately from pictures I'd seen in hunting magazines. They were beautiful birds that would rather run than fly, somewhere between the size of a bobwhite quail and a pheasant. Breakfast was nearly at hand.

My plans did not include anything fancy. I just wanted to pop a couple of them in the head with the .22 so we'd have something to eat. Buster picked one out and fired. A puff of dust rose behind the bird. "You shot too high," I offered, just as his second shot did the same. "You gotta aim lower," I urged as the third shot also went awry.

By now the chukars were getting more than a little edgy. "Give me the gun," I demanded. Buster obliged. I think we both had a hand on the rifle when it went off, sending a hollow point bullet into the center of my right foot.

For a split second, it was eerily quiet and calm, as it always is in times of unexpected shock or horror. I was still coming to grips with my plight when the pain hit, and I knew I was in big trouble. The next town on Highway 87 was Dalhart, about 30 miles ahead. Buster put his foot in the carburetor and Lynn tried his best to comfort me as we sped toward the first available hospital.

The streets were deserted when we entered Dalhart. It was early Sunday morning and the little town was still asleep. Buster and Lynn found the hospital and carried me in. A nurse met us and was almost as shocked as we were. When she recovered from her momentary dither, she led us to the emergency room and told my attendants to lay me down on my back on the shiny stainless steel table. Every time my heart beat, it felt like I was getting shot all over again. I begged her to give me something for the pain. She told me that she couldn't give me anything until the doctor authorized it. "Well, where's the doctor?" I groaned.

"At home, I guess," she said.

"You mean we're the only people in this hospital?"

The nurse shrugged.

Eventually I convinced her to call the good doctor. She made the call, and I waited. After 30 minutes and still no doctor, I asked where the doctor lived. "Next door to the hospital," she replied.

"You mean after 30 minutes he can't make it to this hospital from next door!" I yelled, incredulous and hurting badly. "Then call him again and tell him I need something for this pain!"

Buster and Lynn made a valiant effort to divert my attention with a bunch of lame jokes I had already heard. All jokes aside, I needed something for the pain before I went up in a cloud of smoke.

The doctor appeared exactly one hour after the nurse's first call. I already didn't like him, but I was willing to cut him some slack after he authorized a shot of something for the pain. When it kicked in, I became amazingly civil again. After a careful examination and x-rays, the doctor announced, "You have a serious gunshot wound to your right foot."

That was the last straw. In spite of the pain medication, which was suddenly wearing off, I retorted, "You've got to be kidding! What is the charge for this information?"

"Seventy-five dollars," he said.

"If that's what I have to pay you for a diagnosis that I already know, then I'm darned sure I can't afford your cure!"

With that I told Buster and Lynn to drag me back to the car. The doctor ran along behind us, telling me that I couldn't leave ... something about all gunshot wounds having to be reported to and inspected by the police before a patient could be discharged. He was still yelling at us on the sidewalk when we drove out of sight.

"What should we do now?" asked Lynn.

I have no idea why, but I said, "Let's pack it in ice and keep on truckin'."

We found a cardboard box with the top cut off. I cut a u-shaped slot in one of the narrow ends so I could sit crossway on the back seat with my right leg extended and my foot resting in the box. After lining the box with plastic bags, we went to an ice plant and filled our cooler with crushed ice, which we put in plastic bags and packed all around my right foot as needed. For some reason I thought keeping my foot packed in ice would help.

Finances were now a prime concern, especially after doling out $75 to Dr. Dim Bulb. I knew that eventually this foot was going to get expensive, but since my father was a retired military man, I was eligible for free medical care until I turned 21.

There were a lot of miles between Dalhart, Texas, and Santa Maria, California, but the price was right. We kept going.

The only gunshot wounds I had even seen were in cowboy movies. They either poured whisky in the bullet hole or into the mouth of the victim. I wasn't a drinker, so I decided the alcohol would be poured into the wound. We bought a few bottles of rubbing alcohol and several large boxes of gauze. Then, twice each day at our gas stops, the three of us would go into the men's room. Buster and Lynn would unwrap my foot and then do their best to hold me down as they poured alcohol into the bullet hole. In truth it was just like getting shot all over again twice a day. A fresh gauze bandage was applied and we were good for another 300 miles.

My removal from the driving rotation put a lot of pressure on my comrades as they continued the journey west across Utah. I had friends in Lake Tahoe, where we could rest up for free, but Lynn and Buster were wearing down and nodding off at the wheel. They kept rotating drivers, but it was getting dangerous. Finally neither of them could stay awake. I had had plenty of time to sleep in the back seat, so I finally told them to pull over onto the shoulder of Highway 50, a few miles west of Eureka, Nevada. My pals assumed it was naptime, but I had a plan – albeit unconventional – that would keep us moving.

As long as my right foot was elevated, the bleeding subsided, so I figured if I pushed the driver's seat back as far as it would go, and tied my right foot to the rearview mirror, I should be able to drive with my left foot for awhile. There was no traffic on the highway; it seemed plausible to me. Lynn and Buster were too tired to argue. I took the wheel and my comrades fell into long overdue sleep.

Driving across the Nevada desert in the black of night is like being in the twilight zone. There are no landmarks – just endless flat land. The only thing moving that night was the broken yellow stripe in the center of the road as it flickered under the car.

I was lost in time and space when I noticed something. It was a small animal – a rodent of some sort – and I swerved to miss it. However, I felt a faint bump in the undercarriage of the car. Being captivated by all kinds of wildlife, I slowed to a stop, turned the car around and headed back to see if it was still there. I expected that whatever I found would be dead. Then my bleary-eyed buddies awoke, asking what was happening. The critter was lying right on the center strip of the highway. I untied my foot from the rear view mirror and, with the help of my friends, hobbled out to inspect it.

Lo and behold, it was a kit fox – a tiny western species with huge ears. It was a cute little animal of about three or four pounds, which, to our amazement, was still breathing.

We looked for any sign of a wound, but found none. Its head must have made very slight contact with the car – not even enough to break the skin but enough to knock it out. Well, we couldn't leave a perfectly alive fox lying in the middle of the road. We scooped it up and put it on a towel in a small box in the back seat, where it slept quietly for the rest of the night as I drove on toward Lake Tahoe.

By morning we were amidst the mountains. Serious R&R was imminent. Soon we were ascending the eastern slopes of the Sierra Madre past Carson City and finally into Lake Tahoe. Before calling my friend, we stopped to fill up with gas and attend to my foot. I had by then lost enough blood that standing up made me pretty light headed, so we bought a pair of crutches. Our little fox was showing signs of life, too. At first it could sit up and by evening could walk around some, but only in tight circles.

After 24 hours of recuperation in Tahoe, we pointed the car south and began the journey to Santa Maria. I had called my parents and told them I was wounded and heading their way.

We crossed the Nevada/California line, right into a Highway Patrol stop. The officer stuck his head in the car and asked where we were going. "To Santa Maria," we announced with as much nonchalance as we could muster. About that time, the officer spotted the fox in the back seat.

"Whose little guy is that?"

"Oh this is Freddie, my pet fox," I replied.

The officer eyed me suspiciously. “Is he tame?”

“Sure.”

“Do you have a permit for the fox?”

“Oh, yessir I do,” I said. “Buster, look in the glove box and find my permit.”

As Buster began rummaging around in the glove box, feigning a search for a permit that didn’t exist, the officer relaxed and became infatuated with the cute little canine. “Can you pet him?” he asked.

“Uh, sure,” I replied, “He’s really friendly.”

With that, the officer reached through the open window and patted the fox on the head. “Freddie” in turn clamped down on one of his fingers with his razor-sharp teeth.

As the patrolman yanked his bleeding finger back, I jumped in with my best explanation: “Sorry officer, I was just gonna mention that it takes Freddie a little while to warm up to strangers, but he’s really gentle once he gets to know you.”

“Get the heck on down the road,” said our man in blue, which we did with a huge sigh of relief.

I was admitted to the military hospital at Vandenberg Air Force Base and none too soon. Due to blood loss I was having real trouble standing up without passing out. The first order of events after I was admitted was the medical report. The medic came with his pen and hospital forms and began asking me questions:

"What's your name, rank and serial number?"

"Name's Russell Thornberry, but I don't have a rank or serial number."

"If you don't have a rank and serial number, then what are you doing in an Air Force hospital?" he snapped.

"My father is retired military and I'm his dependent - 19 years old," I explained.

Now the medic added some sarcasm to the interrogation. "Well what's your daddy's name, rank and serial number?"

"Admiral Russell Frank Thornberry," I blurted out, "not sure about his serial number, though."

Seeing that look of fear settle in his eyes was a thing of beauty. In fact, my dad had retired a chief petty officer, not an admiral. But I didn't want to spoil the moment.

"What is the nature of your injury?" the medic continued.

"Gunshot wound," I replied.

"Where were you shot?"

I thought the bloody bandage on my right foot was obvious. Call me crazy. So I assumed he must have meant in what geographical location was I shot.

"North of Dalhart, Texas," I answered.

"Then why are you here?"

"Because the treatment is free."

"So let me get this straight. You were shot north of Dalhart, Texas, and you came all the way to Vandenberg to see a doctor?!"

"Yessir."

"So when exactly did you get shot?"

"Guess it was about 4 ½ days ago."

"And what have you been doing since then?"

"I've been driving like crazy! It was a long way here!"

The baffled medic turned on his heels and left without another word.

I found out in the hospital that I had probably been spared gangrene by icing down my foot and pouring alcohol in the bullet hole twice a day. While I wouldn't recommend it to anyone, God was looking after a fool. I still have two feet, although not exactly the same shape and size.

As for Freddie, we released him after he regained his ability to walk in a straight line. He scampered off into the desert evening as if nothing had ever happened.

CHAPTER 15

The Buckwheat Bear

THERE'S AN OLD TIMER'S SAYING for the occasion when a bear is spotted eating grain: "There's a bear in the buckwheat!" Although the wheat mentioned below might not actually be buckwheat, it was wheat nevertheless – and there was a bear in it!

He was a hyper little plastic surgeon from New York.

Told me he was being sued by some woman whose facelift had flopped, which accounted for his nerves. The face-flop lawsuit was worth a million dollars, so the doctor's concern was understandable. In any case, he thought a bear hunt was just what he needed to settle him down, especially if he could find a blond bear that reminded him of the blond woman behind all his grief.

In my hunting area the black bears were in a variety of color phases, including blond. I had seen one particularly large blond bear on several occasions, feeding in a wheat stubble field at the mouth of a large timbered canyon. It appeared that the bear was living in the canyon and coming down in the evening for the wheat. I described the bear to the doctor and he was delighted.

That evening, we motored upstream to the mouth of the canyon, tied up the boat, and climbed up on the bank to inspect the situation. We found a perfect ambush site in a pile of deadfall, downwind from where the bear usually entered the field. I told the doctor to get comfortable and we'd just wait until the bear showed.

This was fine at first, but after a half hour or so, he started to fidget. I could see he was getting restless, but there was no better plan than what we were doing. I pretended not to notice his fidgeting, and that only seemed to make matters worse. Finally he jumped to his feet and snapped, "What kind of fool do you think I am?"

"What are you talking about?" I asked.

"I'm talking about sitting out in the middle of a wheat field, waiting for a bear!" he snorted.

I still wasn't tracking him.

"Since when do bears eat wheat?" he demanded. "I wasn't born yesterday you know ... I've done enough big game hunting to know when I'm being had!"

I was shocked. To this day, I've never seen a black bear that wouldn't eat wheat if he had the chance, and I told the doctor as much. That only made him more irate. His face turned redder and the veins in his neck began to bulge out of his collar. The little doctor was coming unglued right before my eyes. I wondered what on Earth had gotten into him.

He was really tearing a strip off me when I spotted a fresh pile of bear dung on the ground a few feet away. Then the idea struck me. "Hold it, Doc," I interrupted. "You ever seen black bear dung?"

"Of course I've seen black bear dung," he snapped. "What do you take me for ... some greenhorn boy scout?"

"Well, would you say this is bear dung?" I inquired, pointing to the fresh heap.

"Yes," he said, "that's black bear dung. What is this, some kind of quiz?"

"Well, do you notice anything peculiar about it?" I persisted.

"What do you mean?" he asked, puzzled.

I kicked the pile of dung, exposing hundreds of grains of wheat. "How do you suppose all this wheat found its way into this pile of bear dung if bears don't eat wheat?"

He walked up to the pile of fresh bear dung and stared at it skeptically. While he was staring and stammering, I saw movement at the mouth of the canyon. It was the bear. I watched him move out of the timber into the stubble field, chowing down on the kernels of wheat spilled among the stubble. "By the way, Doc," I said casually, "your blond bear is standing right over there if you're still interested."

When the doctor looked up, his eyes popped in disbelief. "That's the blond bear!" he gasped.

"You're absolutely right about that," I replied. "And what do you suppose he's doing over there?"

"How would I know?"

"Well Sir, he's eating wheat, just like I said he would. You wanna shoot 'im?"

"Yes, yes," he said, "I wanna shoot him!"

"Okay, here's the deal. I'll let you shoot the bear on one condition: I won't practice plastic surgery if you'll quit telling me how to guide bear hunters. Is that a deal?"

"Alright, alright," he panted, "just let me take a shot!"

I told him to sit down behind a big log and take a solid rest. The bear was about 250 yards away, which should have been an easy distance for the doctor's .338 Magnum. After much hyperventilating, he finally touched off a shot, and I saw dirt fly, 100 yards on the other side of the bear.

The shot was obviously too high. At the sound of the shot, the bear burned rubber as he headed back up the canyon. The doctor tried two more shots at the bear, on the dead run, but never came close. "Did I get him?" he asked hopefully.

"Don't think so," I replied, "but we'd better go over there and look to be sure."

The doctor was pretty torqued up by then. His nerves, combined with seeing and missing the very bear he came for, had him bouncing like a bag of jumping beans. When we arrived at the spot where the bear had been standing when he shot, there was no blood, no hair, no nothing.

"Well Doc, looks like a clean miss."

"Are you sure this is where he was standing?" he asked.

"Yep, I'm sure it was here," I replied.

"How can you be so sure?" he insisted.

"Well, here's all the proof I need," I said, pointing down to a steaming heap of wheat-filled bear dung. "This pile is just barely on the ground. Maybe you'd like to take this home with you as a souvenir?"

CHAPTER 16

The Woodland Park Massacre

My wife Sharleen and I were sitting in our home office in Woodland Park, Colo., when we heard a loud crunching sound in the wall. Suddenly our Internet cratered, so I assumed that something had crunched its way through some wiring. I called the Internet provider and they promised to send a technician out right away.

The following day he showed up in his little white van and began asking questions about the wiring. Since I was only leasing the house, I had no idea about it. He checked some electrical outlets and asked if we had a basement. I explained that there was a cellar where the heating system was located but that I had never been in it.

"Where is it?" he asked.

I led him into the master bedroom, through the bathroom, and into the walk-in closet. At the back of the closet, I lifted up the piece of the floor that doubled as the cellar door and pointed at the dark hole below.

“”Here it is,” I said, “but I’ve never been down there.”

He peered into the darkness and asked if there was a light down there.

I didn’t know.

With that, he started down the little 2x4 ladder and disappeared.

I was bent over, looking into the black hole and wondering what the technician might find, when a furry cannonball shot out of the hole and grabbed me by the throat. In shock and horror, I screamed like a little girl and started backing out of the closet, ripping at the creature with both hands until I freed his grip and pitched him away. It was a huge fox squirrel – presumably the culprit that had chewed through my wiring. He was bouncing off the closet walls at warp speed.

By any means possible, I had to make sure he didn’t get into the house. I spun back into the bathroom, as did the squirrel, still ricocheting. Hand-to-hand combat was no good; I needed a weapon and quick. I took a deep breath, opened the bathroom door, jumped out and slammed it shut, trapping the demon muncher. Next I ran through the house in search of anything with which to do combat. I spotted a broom in the kitchen and grabbed it, unscrewed the handle, and headed back to the master bathroom.

Another deep breath and in I went. I took my brave stance, like Mickey Mantle at the plate. Every time the squirrel bounced my way, I took a swing at him. But he was fast – really fast – and I was always just a hair behind him. My adrenaline was off the charts as the air sizzled.

Numerous swings later, I began to tire, wondering if I was going to have to rethink the weaponry.

Then the squirrel made a mistake.

He bounced off the wall above the toilet and landed on the shower curtain, which offered no resistance when he tried to jump again. The pause was for only a millisecond, but I instinctively swung at him with all the strength I had. I centered him!

That was the good news.

The bad news was that I hit him with so much force that he literally exploded. Squirrel blood and guts covered the bathroom walls and me and my "Louisville Slugger" broom handle. I stood there gasping for breath and wiping the goo from my face, trying to process the horrific conditions of my bathroom, when the closet door opened. The serviceman stood frozen in fear. For an instant I was shocked by the horror in his eyes. Then I realized that I was the source of his horror. I started my breathless explanation of what had just happened, but he had no interest in hearing it. The poor guy ran like a jackrabbit to his van and roared down the driveway in a cloud of dust and gravel, never to be seen again.

My son Darren soon came by the house and found the whole episode too hilarious to believe. Like most of the "beyond belief" happenings in my life, I can now see the humor in it, too.

I mentioned to Darren that when I was a kid we regularly ate fox squirrels and that I preferred them to cottontail rabbits.

"How do they taste?" my son asked.

Well, since I had a prime candidate for the skillet still in the bathtub, I cooked it up for him. He admitted that it was pretty good.

Eventually another serviceman came and fixed my squirrel-chewed wiring. I didn't dare ask him if he had spoken to the first guy.

CHAPTER 17

The Saga of the Iron Bowl Doe

AS I RECALL, ONLY TWICE in my life have I set out to shoot a "nice, fat doe" for meat. It's not that I have taken only two does for meat; it's just that the others were taken incidentally, while hunting for bucks. Those "other" does were taken without incident, but something sinister occurs in the universe when I decide to specifically shoot a doe for meat.

EXAMPLE A

A friend at the office who knew I wanted a meat doe said he had the perfect place only 10 minutes from work. From the advertised treestand, I could shoot does until I ran out of arrows and they would just keep coming. Or so he said.

"Perfect," I thought. I didn't want to make a major endeavor of it, so this place sounded great. Charlie even offered to be my guide to the world's most productive doe stand.

We met before daybreak. Once parked, Charlie led the way in the pitch dark through the jungle-like undergrowth and green briar vines that grow abundantly in central Alabama (ripping deer hunters to shreds). I was trying to un-impale myself from a green briar vine that had me by the throat when Charlie let go of a branch that snapped back and slapped me square in my right eye. Immediately that eye started looking like a blood red hard-boiled egg. I followed Charlie with my good eye until he finally admitted he was totally lost. At that point we abandoned the search for the world's greatest doe stand and began searching for the Toyota. In the end, the nice, fat doe remained safer than a day in jail and all these years later I still have a bloodshot right eye. Nice fat doe – 1. Russell – 0.

I tell you this to set the stage for "Example B." Bad stuff happens to people. It's a fact of life. But it's not until it happens a second time that one stops and considers the possibility of a trend. Enter nice, fat doe Number 2.

Example B

Saturday, Nov. 19, 2005 – 3 p.m.

I had been bowhunting a very likely "unlikely spot" 30 miles from my home in Montgomery. It was a narrow 65-acre strip of planted pines bordered on one side by a rural highway and on the other by the adjacent property's hardwoods. There was a narrow open corridor along my side of the fence providing the all-important "edge" that whitetails frequent.

I put my stand 20 feet high in a lone water oak overlooking the edge between the pines and the hardwoods. The planted pines were a perfect whitetail bedding area. The distance from my treestand to the highway was only 200 yards. I could hear traffic and could even see the tops of the 18-wheelers. I picked this noisy spot because it was precisely the kind of place that most hunters would not like. My rationale was that mature bucks often seek out places where you would least expect them to be, providing they have ample cover.

Oh, did I mention that there was a little airstrip right across the highway and I could also watch small aircraft take off and land? As I said – it was a very likely unlikely spot. In five previous trips, I had consistently seen one mature doe and a yearling. The doe was the most secretive deer I have ever seen.

On this afternoon I decided to try to shoot this doe for meat. She was more of a challenge than most trophy bucks, and my venison supply from the previous season was depleted.

When I arrived at camp headquarters I was amazed to find myself alone. Then it dawned on me that it was Iron Bowl Saturday. Auburn and Alabama were playing that afternoon and every red blooded Alabamian was either at the game or sitting in front of a television. I, a transplanted Texan, didn't have a dog in that fight, so I was destined to have the woods to myself.

At 4 p.m. the doe came slinking through the pines. I could see that she would cross the narrow edge opening about 24 yards from my tree. I was ready. When she stepped clear of the pines and looked both ways, I slipped my arrow through her boiler room. She bolted, but I knew there was meat on the table.

I found her piled up in some green briars and shin-tangle. It was dark when I finished dragging her back to my truck, parked in the ditch, right beside the highway. After loading her into the truck bed, I unlocked the passenger side door and loaded my day pack, bow, quiver, etc., in the back seat, pushed the unlock button to unlock the driver's side door, tossed my keys onto the center console, slammed the passenger side door, and walked around the truck to open the driver's side door.

Apparently I only thought I had pushed the unlock button. In fact, I had pushed the wrong end of said button.

The goods news was that I had the woods all to myself since it was Iron Bowl Saturday. That was also the bad news. There was no one at camp headquarters to help me. I was 30 miles from home, all dressed up with nowhere to go.

"Okay Russell," I said to myself, "you have to think your way out of this. Let's see how innovative you can be in a pinch."

"First I must consider my options," I replied. An examination of truck entry options spelled a broken window, no matter how I sliced it. My windshield was the obvious choice, since it was already cracked in a couple of places. The truth was that

I had intended to have it replaced by then. If not for procrastination it would have been a brand new windshield. Wow, let's hear it for procrastination!

Next was to find the required break-and-enter tool. An examination of my truck bed revealed yet more fruit of fortuitous procrastination – a garden hoe that I'd meant to put back in my tool shed. More kudos for procrastination. At last my lifestyle was paying off.

The hoe won the break-and-enter tool contest by default. The concept was to stand on the front bumper of the truck and bash a hole in the windshield with the butt end of the hoe. "Thornberry, you're a genius," I thought as I climbed up on the front bumper.

The first bash bounced off with no effect whatsoever. It wasn't going to be as easy as I'd thought. I took a deep breath, steadied my balance, reared back with the hoe and drove it against the glass just as a car whizzed by. I couldn't help but notice the scowls and the noses pressed against the windows. Suddenly I felt very conspicuous and guilty. More cars passed, their occupants sneering. Unfortunately they went by me too fast for me to explain my plight, and I didn't know a fast enough sign language to prove my innocence. But some of the folks did figure out a one-finger salute to express their distaste for what they supposed I was doing.

Once the self-consciousness subsided, I was back to the task at hand. I pummeled the windshield again and again until I finally blasted a hoe handle-sized hole through its middle. Of course the entire windshield was then a virtual jigsaw puzzle of cracks, which made it impossible for me to see through. I shined my flashlight through the hole. There, on the console, were the keys to my freedom. Now, how to get them through the hole?

I envisioned a long thin stick with a hook on the end that I could thread through the hole and hook into the key ring without the keys falling off and out of my sight.

First I had to find just the right stick, approximately five feet long. I found a dead pine limb and stripped it of its tiny branches until I had the perfect stick. Then I found another smaller pine branch and stripped all but one branch. The remaining branch, which angled toward the tip of the limb to which it was attached, was to be my hook. I lashed it to the main pole with one of my boot laces so that the small 2-inch branch at the tip was pointing backward like a crude hook.

With tension that begged for a thunderous drum roll, I eased the limb through the hole, gingerly slipped the hook through the key ring and eased my keys out of the truck.

Success!

"MacGyver has nothing on you, Thornberry," I chuckled aloud. As I proudly opened the driver's side door and climbed in, my pride took a sudden nose-dive. The cab was covered in broken glass, the facing of my dashboard was peeled off, my electronic rear view mirror was lying on the floorboard and there was a very impressive hole gouged through the top of the dashboard. That little inner voice whispered again, "Thornberry, this is going to be expensive."

Understatement!

The bill read like this:
New windshield: $350
New electronic mirror: $450
Patch hole in dashboard: $150
Co-Pay for Dr. visit: $25
Prescription poison ivy ointment: $60
(I got poison ivy on my hands from the doe's legs when I dragged her out of the pines, then rubbed the sweat from my eyes. You know the rest.)
Meat processing fee: $43.65
Total: $1,078.65.

If I ever again feel the need to go out and shoot a nice, fat doe for meat, I'll go straight to the supermarket and buy 100 pounds of prime filet mignon and 50 pounds of fresh lobster tails for a fraction of the cost of the world's most expensive doe.

Postscript:

Auburn beat Alabama that day, and I shot a nice, fat doe. But like the University of Alabama, scoring a few points winneth not the game. By any measure of a contest, the Iron Bowl doe emerged victorious. Every time I open my freezer I am reminded of my painful defeat.

CHAPTER 18

Once in a Blue Moon

WITH A 10-DAY BUSINESS TRIP looming, I really wanted to go bowhunting. But I knew I shouldn't. Too much work to do. Then Tracy, the office manager, remarked, "Wow, tonight we have a blue moon!"

A blue moon! Suddenly my resolve to work and not bowhunt was weakening. I had been getting regular trail cam pictures of a real nice 8-pointer for a couple of weeks. Maybe the blue moon was an omen – the key to putting an arrow in him on my first bowhunt of the season. "Sure would make a great story," I thought.

After all, I am a storyteller, right?

Something inside me said, "You need to stay home … this is not practical."

So I did what I usually do when common sense collides with impulse: I ignored it.

By 6 p.m. I was in my treestand in a tall spruce. The property was private and I was conditionally allowed to hunt there so long as I did not take a motorized vehicle there under any circumstances. I agreed because it meant there would be no 4-wheelers racing around while I was trying to hunt. (Where I live, Hells Angels have traded their Harleys for quads and they seem to delight in destroying everything in their path.) I was delighted to hunt where there was some peace and quiet.

As the sun settled like a soft golden blanket on the treetops and the light dimmed, a few does and a couple of fawns dribbled out of the timber to feed. I didn't expect the buck to show until nearly dark. There were no more than 15 minutes of shooting time left when I spotted him easing through the timber like a dark shadow. "Wow," I thought, "This blue moon thing is working out like a charm!"

His tall rack, still in velvet, looked even larger than on my trail cam photos. I assumed my shooting position 25 feet above him and waited for him to step into the clear. After a few minutes behind a clump of small spruce trees, he walked out in front of me, broadside. What luck. The shot was perfect and I had my first Blue Moon Buck! What a story this was going to make!

A short tracking job confirmed my shot. I set up a little tripod, mounted it to my camera, set the timer and jumped back and forth from camera to deer until I finally got a photo that had both of us in it. By then it was 9:30 p.m. and the work was just getting started.

Since I was not allowed to take a motor vehicle onto the property, I had a little deer cart in the back of my truck where I had parked it beside the highway about half mile away. I sent a text message to my bride to inform her of my success and that I would be home late. That, dear reader, was an understatement. By the time I retrieved the cart from my truck and loaded the deer on it, along with my bow, daypack, etc., it was pushing 11 p.m.

Hauling the loaded cart through thick timber, over deadfall and rough ground, was exhausting, so I paused periodically to catch my breath and remind myself what a great idea it had been to go hunting. "It's a small price to pay for such a fine buck, especially on a blue moon," I reasoned.

It was after midnight when I reached the barbed wire fence bordering the highway and dragged the buck, the cart, and my gear across it. I was really pooped, but grateful, to have completed my grand adventure.

My truck was about 40 yards away, but I was quite finished dragging that deer. I simply walked to the truck, unlocked it and started backing toward the deer and gear in the ditch behind me. Suddenly, I heard a loud whooshing sound. My command of the obvious told me that something had gone very, very wrong.

I hit the brakes, exited the truck and walked to the rear from where the mystery whoosh had originated. My initial assessment about going hunting on a blue moon suddenly came back to me: "This could be very good or it could be very bad."

Or it could be both.

I had backed over the tip of the buck's right main beam, anchoring it to the ground and forcing the next point through the sidewall of my right rear tire. Thus the whoosh I heard as all the air formerly contained therein escaped into the chilly night air. It was 12:30 a.m.

Next came the chilling realization that I had no jack or tire tool in the truck. "Guess it's time to call my bride," I thought. "She isn't going to be impressed."

No answer on the cell phone so I called the landline. It rang and rang. She was already asleep.

To say that a rural highway in central western Alberta was empty and devoid of all vehicle traffic would be an understatement. I sat in my truck for a while, considering my options – no, make that my option – which was a long walk home.

"But what if someone comes along and burgles my truck?" I reasoned. "And I can't lock the tailgate on the topper so the burglar would not only find my abandoned truck, but my Blue Moon Buck and my deer cart, and my bow and ..."

I realized that I was going to have to pull the buck back uphill, out of the ditch, back under the fence and into the timber where a passerby wouldn't find it. But then there was the problem of coyotes finding him before daylight. So I covered the buck with my camo jacket and my safety vest, assuming that the human scent would ward off predators. Next came the deer cart and all my gear, back into the timber from whence it came. Time: 1:15 a.m.

My cell phone battery was seconds away from dying, so in a last ditch effort for rescue, I texted Sharleen four words: "Flat tire. Am walking."

My hope was that somewhere in what remained of the night she might realize that I was missing and check her cell phone. I doubted that she would find the circumstances surrounding my dilemma amusing at that hour, so I didn't bother with details.

High top rubber boots are something less that ideal for walking down the middle of the highway. "Ker-flop, ker-flop," they blubbered as I marched eastward, trying to stay positive.

On the brighter side, that huge Blue Moon lit up the lonely highway so at least I could see.

Later that night, or perhaps I should say early that morning, as the novelty of marching down a dark highway was wearing off, what to my wondering eyes should appear, but a distant set of headlights. "Dear Lord," I prayed, "Please let that be Sharleen!"

When the car drew near, it slowed to a stop in the middle of the highway and the driver's side window rolled down.

"What a fortuitous moment," I thought.

"Get your butt in this car," snapped my bride. I obliged without comment and we drove home in blissful silence. I'm quite sure that this could only happen once in a Blue Moon.

CHAPTER 19

The Ultimate Decoy

MY OFFICE PHONE AT BUCKMASTERS rang just as I was getting ready to go film a bowhunt in Kansas. The gent on the line was a stranger who wanted to tell me about a super whitetail decoy he had invented. I got lots of calls from inventors, hoping to get some publicity for their products, in those days. This call was no different, but the product was a buck decoy that, according to the inventor, could twitch its tail from side to side as well as rotate its ears.

I had used deer decoys a time or two when hunting where they were legal, and I knew the value of that side-to-side tail twitch, which is the "all clear" sign in whitetail body language. I had even entertained the idea of trying to add such tail movement to a decoy to make it more lifelike and less threatening to other deer. The problem with decoys is that they are so rigid and statuesque that they scare away does like crazy. They get worried when they try to see what they think the decoy is staring at, especially when they can't figure it out. All that is to say that I saw merit in this decoy.

The designer had built in small, battery-driven motors to twitch the tail and rotate the ears. The user could set them in motion remotely with a small control box like the ones used to operate remote-controlled toy cars. Kansas allowed the use of decoys, so I told the inventor to ship his prototype to Kansas. I would try it out and let him know what I thought of it.

Buckmasters cameraman Jimmy Little and I arrived a few days later in the Flint Hills of eastern Kansas to begin our hunt with renowned bowhunter Dale Larson. I couldn't imagine a better guide or a better property to hunt.

The Flint Hills were most contradictory to the type of terrain I expected to find in Kansas, which I assumed was all just flat open grasslands. Not so. Instead, this was steep and grassy, pocked by deep timbered ravines.

In his scouting, Dale had already identified two or three record class bucks, which raised our expectations, but as quickly as they were raised Mother Nature began doing all within her power to lower them. Dreadful heat made way for torrential rain and thunderstorms powered by gale force winds, which made for impossible hunting conditions. The deer had nowhere to go, but staying in our treestands with lightning cracking and limbs snapping was too risky. We gave it our best shot for a couple of days. During that time, we only saw one doe, chased by someone's farm dog. Bummer!

Four nights later, the rain finally stopped and the fog set in. The next morning it felt as though we could wring water out of the air. Even at that it was the best hunting weather we had encountered, so with the clock ticking away our six hunting days we dutifully set out in the damp darkness of early morning with the decoy in tow.

The plan was to set up near a fence crossing where four major ravines funneled deer out of the timber onto converging trails no more than 30 yards from our stand. We were tucked into a thicket of small oaks and cedars with a deep ravine at our backs. Jimmy was in a 15-foot tripod stand that gave an over-the-shoulder view of me in a treestand in a small oak. We placed the decoy about 20 yards in front of us, flanking a trail where any deer that entered the little clearing would be sure to see it.

After setting up the decoy, I climbed up into my treestand and picked up the little control box to give it a try. I pressed the on button and twisted the toggle stick. Even in the dim, predawn light I could see the decoy's tail twitch from side to side. "Killer," Jimmy giggled from behind me. I tried the ears and they rotated so realistically that I had to chuckle to myself. No buck on Earth could see this electronic marvel and resist. The rut was just getting underway, and the bucks had already been through their posturing and fighting to establish dominance. Now, if they encountered a buck they hadn't yet come to terms with, it would be the essence of their nature to challenge this newcomer. The trap was set. Jimmy and I were optimistic once again.

About 10 minutes passed and the light was still quite dim in the heavy fog.

"Big buck," Jimmy hissed, "over on the hillside!"

I could barely see his silhouette, but what I could see was enough to convince me that this had to be one of those record book deer Dale had told us about. The trail he was on wouldn't bring him into bow range, so it was time to get proactive. Now we would see if this decoy was all it was cracked up to be!

"Film this if you can," I whispered to Jimmy. "I'm going to use the decoy."

I heard the faint hum of the camera. We were rolling. I turned the on switch and twisted the tail toggle. At first nothing happened.

"Please!" I whispered to the decoy. "If you're ever going to work, do it now!"

I twisted the tail toggle a bit farther and at last the tail began to move – side to side at first and then, picking up momentum, it began to spin like a propeller. Suddenly it was spinning so hard I thought it was actually going to pull the decoy backwards. At that point the ears also began rotating in complete circles, too. I frantically mashed the off button, but it wouldn't work. This decoy had a mind of its own and there was nothing I could do to stop it.

I frantically glanced over at the buck, hoping that somehow he had not seen the circus, but it was too late. He was standing stone still, staring at the decoy in utter disbelief. A few seconds later, he threw his tail in the air and sped off quick as lightning.

Meanwhile, back at the decoy from hell, the show was still going. The control box was useless. The thick wet fog had caused a short in the wiring. I climbed out of my stand, ran out to the decoy and began pulling out every wire I could find until his propeller tail and revolving ears were finally motionless. Then I carried him back to our stands and buried him under some brush.

We saw no more giants on that trip, but I did finally arrow a 140-ish 10-point buck on the last day, which would have been a showstopper in most places. Alas, he was "just a buck" by Kansas standards.

As I reflect on that crazy morning I am reminded that those giant bucks lead charmed lives. That monster we saw in the fog that morning might be the only white-tailed buck in America to have had his life saved by the "ultimate" decoy. Ugh!

CHAPTER 20

Dances with Turtles

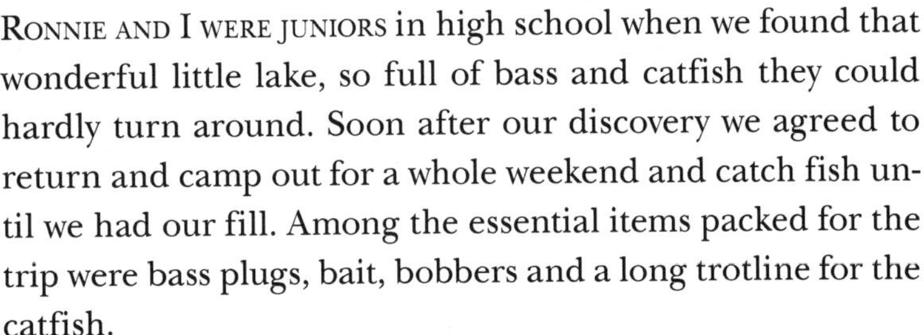

RONNIE AND I WERE JUNIORS in high school when we found that wonderful little lake, so full of bass and catfish they could hardly turn around. Soon after our discovery we agreed to return and camp out for a whole weekend and catch fish until we had our fill. Among the essential items packed for the trip were bass plugs, bait, bobbers and a long trotline for the catfish.

We could concentrate on bass fishing while the trotline handled the catfish. And we would take along my little 10-foot plywood barge for running the trotline. It was originally designed to haul duck decoys when I waded into the salt marshes along the Texas Gulf Coast, but I was sure it was stable enough to hold Ronnie and me. I even added a little transom so we could use Ronnie's 2-horse Johnson outboard.

When the appointed weekend arrived, we were wildly excited. First we pitched the tent and made a livable camp, then we went bass fishing. Bass were plentiful, as expected, and we caught so many fish we were delirious. After a banquet of hotdogs and beans, we agreed it was time to set out the trotline. It would take us about an hour to get it set, and after that we would fish for bass again until dark.

The trotline was 200 yards long and was set up with a lead line and hook about every six feet. We baited some of the lines with liver and some with cut bait, feeling confident that by sunup there should be a catfish on every hook. The plywood barge was a little tippy, but as long as we stayed fairly centered it worked okay. The little outboard pushed us along just fine. What a wonderful idea! After trotline duties were complete, we resumed bass fishing until dark.

At dawn I poked my head out of the tent and looked out at the trotline. It was no longer visible. Obviously the weight of all the catfish had dragged it deep into the lake! Wow, what a way to start a day – with enough catfish already on the line to sink the Queen Mary! Ronnie and I set a new record for quickly jumping into blue jeans and sneakers.

Ronnie filled the tiny gas tank in the top of the outboard motor while I grabbed a pair of pliers and a stringer. Then, perched cautiously in the middle of the barge, we headed for open water to reap the bounty of the good Earth. We picked up the trotline where it was tied to the willow tree on our side of the lake. Ronnie stayed at the helm, giving us just enough gas to move us slowly forward. I kneeled over the bow and followed the line, hand over hand, out to deeper water. When we came to the first hook, we were rewarded with a fat 3-pound channel cat.

"Can you believe this?" I chortled. "And this is just the first hook. We're gonna have to make several trips to haul all these fish back."

Ronnie was equally excited. We eased forward to the next hook. The trotline was getting heavier under the weight of more fish, and the farther from shore we went, the more I had to struggle to lift the line up to the barge. But it was a true labor of love. Catfish after catfish went onto the stringer. Seldom was there an empty hook, and those that were had been stripped of their bait. This was truly catfish heaven.

After pulling a four-pounder off the trotline, I could feel the powerful lunging of a heavy fish on the line ahead. "Hey Ronnie, we've got a monster on up ahead," I warned. "He's yanking on this line like crazy."

"Whaddaya think he'll weigh?" Ronnie cackled.

"I dunno, but I wouldn't be surprised if he goes 30 pounds!"

"Think you can handle him alright?" Ronnie asked.

"Ain't no catfish ever been hatched I can't handle," I bragged. The closer we got to the fish, the more he fought. I tried to pull him up, but he fought his way back down time after time.

"How we doin' up there?" came Ronnie's voice from the stern. I was lying chest-down on the barge for extra stability, with my head and shoulders hanging over the bow. For every foot I gained, the huge fish pulled the line back through my hands, sometimes so fast that the trotline burned my fingers. To complicate matters somewhat, a wind was coming up, which kept blowing the barge away from the trotline. So, in addition to my struggle to subdue a large, powerful catfish, I was now also struggling to hold the barge in position with the trotline. Ronnie was trying to stay balanced in the stern while holding the stringer and taking the catfish from me as I unhooked them. The choppier water was making his job more difficult.

"I can't hold the barge in position and fight this crazy catfish, too!" I finally conceded. "Start the motor and see if you can hold us in position!"

Ronnie had to tie the stringer to the side of the barge to free his hands so he could start the motor. We had a dozen or so channel cats on the stringer. Finally he cranked up the 2-horse and nosed us into the wind. Little waves were now breaking over the bow and soaking me. "Keep 'er steady," I sputtered as I rose to my knees. I'd been wrestling with this fish for nearly 10 minutes, but I didn't seem to be gaining ground.

Ronnie couldn't help me because if he came forward the little plywood barge would stand on its nose and we'd both end up in the lake. Exasperation finally turned to anger. I'd had just about enough of this catfish. He was coming aboard whether he liked it or not. "Okay, hold 'er steady now, Ronnie. This fish is about to meet his maker. By the way, did we bring a club with us?"

"Never thought of it," Ronnie replied.

I leaned as far forward as I dared and hauled back on the trotline. The surging weight of the fish resisted and the bow tipped slightly downward. I wrapped the line twice around my right hand so that it couldn't slip backward. Then, reaching down to my shoulder in the water, I grabbed the trotline with my left hand and heaved upward again. I felt the fish lift for the first time. He was tiring at last. "Here he comes!" I cried. "Get ready, Ronnie. He's comin' aboard."

Ronnie was unusually silent, probably preoccupied with trying to keep the barge in position. The wind was now creating small white-capped waves, which were breaking and washing over the deck. We were both soaked, but amidst the adventure of it all, we hardly noticed. I could feel the fish's surrender as I hauled up on the line. He was finally going with the flow, coming up as fast as I could gather line. In fact, faster! I couldn't feel his weight at all now. "He must be swimming right to me!" I yelled.

"Great!" Ronnie crowed in anticipation. "I can hardly wait to see this fish!"

For an instant I held slack line in my hands, wondering if the big catfish had gotten off the line after all that work. My question was answered in a heartbeat. A huge algae-green head erupted from the muddy waters, snapping and hissing at everything in sight.

"Oh God!" I screamed. "It's a giant snapping turtle!" With those words, my life shifted into slow motion. If speed were ever of the essence, it was then, but no matter how I tried to hurry, every movement seemed strangely restrained and animated. I felt like someone trying to Jitterbug to the Tennessee Waltz.

My adversary, on the other hand, seemed to move with blinding speed. The great killer turtle was hooked in the front of his upper jaw, which appeared as a huge, muddy, barnacle-covered beak made of stone – like something left over from the dinosaur era. His softball-sized head shot like lightning from his corrugated shell, extending at least three feet every time he struck, like some evil serpent. His tiny black eyes raged in their muddy sockets. He looked like a culmination of the best creative juices of Hitchcock and Spielberg. Armor plated and invincible, this was the creature of ultimate death and destruction.

I was clearly the source of this man-eating turtle's discontent. At first sight of the turtle's head as it snapped at my face, I recoiled and found myself competing with Ronnie for a place to stand in the stern of the now rollicking barge. "Ya gotta go forward!" he screamed, as the nose of the barge pointed skyward.

Instinctively I pounced back on the bow to bring the nose down before the barge flipped over on its back. The trotline was still cinched around my right hand, and only five feet farther down the line was the killer snapping turtle, which was snapping large chunks of plywood out of the side of our vessel. The wind was blowing harder, pulling the barge farther away from the trotline. The problem was that I was bound to the killer turtle with the trotline, and as the barge drifted farther from the trotline, it was about to pull me off the deck and into the water.

That would have meant certain death. I could see myself being snapped into a million tiny pieces by the razor sharp, steel-trap jaws of the turtle, transformed into an instant feast for a lake full of hungry catfish. What a bizarre end it would be. I felt like Captain Ahab, lashed to Moby Dick, about to go under for the last time.

“Full steam ahead!” I screeched to Ronnie. He gunned the little outboard and it sputtered ahead, buying me time. As the barge surged, it crossed the trotline, entangling the stringer of catfish. Now the stringer was snared in the trotline at one end, and I was still in a “can’t let go” situation with the killer turtle at the other. The turtle, in the meantime, was trying to crawl aboard. His bid to become one of the crew created some logistical problems. Ronnie and I had to alternate kicking the turtle in the rear of his shell to knock him back into the water. To facilitate this fancy footwork, one person had to serve as a human target in front of the turtle to keep him occupied while the other crewmember dashed in from the rear and booted him back into the drink. Not only did this require precise timing and choreography on the kicker’s part, but it also necessitated some phenomenal balancing skills to keep the barge from capsizing. It was a dance to behold, and all the while the turtle was doing his dead-level best to eat both dancers. “Turn us into the wind if you can!” I screamed. “I’ve gotta get enough slack to unwind this line from my hand so I can turn this turtle loose!”

Ronnie, only too willing to oblige, gave the little outboard full throttle. As he did, the gas cap toppled off the top of the motor, allowing gas to spill out on the deck, as the barge rocked and rolled against the waves. Then, a spark from the single sparkplug ignited the spilling gas, and suddenly we had a whole new set of problems.

Yes, we were still attached to a man-eating snapping turtle, which had chomped its way through the sideboard of the barge. And yes, we were engaged in a death-defying balancing act to avoid falling directly into the jaws of death. And now, to add a new element of intrigue to our disintegrating adventure, we were on fire!

"WE'RE BURNING!" came the strained voice from the stern. "WE'RE GONNA DIE OUT HERE!" Those words of encouragement were followed by a loud splash, and I had the overwhelming impression that the aforementioned problems were now mine and mine alone. A quick glance over my shoulder confirmed my suspicion. Ronnie had taken the plunge to freedom. While I didn't really blame him, I admit to some fleeting feelings of contempt. Waves, now larger than ever, broke over the bow, flushing gas and flames to and fro. Even the killer turtle was heading for deep water. Schwartz's Law had taken over. (That's the law that says Murphy was an optimist.) At least Captain Ahab went to his watery grave with dignity. Being lashed to a giant whale was sounding better all the time. I danced feverishly around the deck, sidestepping blue flames. It was either burn with the ship or go hand to hand with the killer turtle in the water. The choice was purely academic. In the end, no matter which I chose, my destiny was clear. I was about to become fish food. The trotline was so tightly wrapped around my fingers that they were turning purple from lack of circulation. If I could just gain enough slack in the trotline to free my hand ...

With all the strength I possessed, I heaved back on the trotline, pulling the nose of the barge right under the waves. I was now knee deep in the water, though still standing on deck. The world stopped under the stress of the moment while boy and turtle held their ground. Suddenly the tension on the trotline broke and I cartwheeled backwards into the lake. I freed my fingers and swam for all I was worth. I was nearly to the shore when I heard Ronnie cheering, "Way to go! I knew you could do it!"

"Do what?" I gasped. "Drown or be burned alive or eaten by that stupid turtle?"

"Aw heck," he said, offering me his hand. "I knew you'd figure something out."

"Thanks for your vote of confidence," I grumbled as I sloshed ashore. "I'll tell ya what I figured out. I figured out that if that turtle hadn't busted that trotline lead, I'd be barbecued fish food right now!"

"Uh, speaking of fish," Ronnie mumbled, after a brief pause, "how we gonna get our stringer of catfish back?"

We stared for a moment at the smoldering barge, still bouncing on the waves. "It's still hung up on the trotline, isn't it?" Ronnie asked.

"Yep, looks like it to me."

Well," he said, "since the turtle's gone, when the fire goes out we could swim back out there and get 'em, couldn't we?"

"Not WE," I assured him. I wasn't going back into that water for any catfish, barge, or anything else. We silently contemplated the situation until a new and more practical plan was born. One of us could walk to the other side of the lake and untie the opposite end of the trotline. Then the two of us could pull it in from our side of the lake.

The plan worked. We recovered our parched plywood barge, our stringer of catfish, and another dozen catfish still on the trotline. Afterward we felt much better about life. After loading up our gear (minus one torched, war-ravaged barge) in the back of Ronnie's pickup, two weary fishermen headed home.

"I can't believe all the stuff that happened out there," Ronnie said wistfully. I nodded in sleepy agreement.

"You could write quite a story about something like that, couldn't you?"

"Yeah, I guess," I nodded. "But who'd believe it?"

CHAPTER 21

The Last Mountain Pony

WHEN MY SON DARREN WAS 12 years old, he accompanied me on a moose hunt in the Yukon. During the hunt, we both were subjected to some of the lowest forms of equine. Our respective horses, "Sinatra" and "Bone Head," did their best to kill us. When that didn't work, they settled for making our daily lives a Horse Hell on Earth. Resultant of that grand experience back in 1987, I swore that there would never again be horseflesh between my knees, unless, of course, in a can of dog food.

When the opportunity came to take Darren back to the Yukon for his own moose hunt in September 2004, the lake hunts were already booked. Those were the civilized trips in which hunters travel in small boats and look for moose or likely places where they might be hiding. In no case are horses used on lake hunts and thus they are my obvious preference.

The only option was a remote horse hunt, but what about my 1987 promise to myself?

Though I still bore the physical and emotional scars from previous rodeos, I broke it and signed on for another chapter of brutal punishment in a bid to make the hunt possible for Darren.

I am aware that some horse aficionados might end up with their panties in a wad because of what I am about to report, but in spite of that I will tell the truth.

The floatplane skimmed through glassy water to a small dock on the shores of Tadru Lake. We bailed out and unloaded our hunting gear. This was the staging area for our hunt, and the horses were all tied up. Duffel bags were sorted and stuffed into panairds. When everything was loaded, we were introduced to our respective steeds. Mine was a chestnut bay named Luci (short for Lucifer). I knew I had to come to terms with the beast, so I sort of snuggled up to her and whispered some sweet nothings in her ear and gave her a quick kiss on the lips. I just wanted her to know that I was at least willing to be friends. She winked back at me.

The remainder of the day was spent in the saddle, ascending ever higher into the wild and remote mountains of the central Yukon. We spent the first night at the relatively comfortable base camp perched on the shoulder of a huge red willow valley where moose were known to dine. The following morning, accompanied by guide Scott Fontaine and his father, Grant, Darren and I mounted our ponies and headed upward again – this time to the Little Mountain spike camp, tucked deep into the green timber five miles below the far side of a high mountain pass. On morning number three we mounted up once more and rode back to the mountain pass where we glassed for moose. We saw caribou, but no moose.

A cutting wind blasted us up on the pass, making the cold unbearable, so Scott finally suggested we ride in search of a fresh bull moose track in the knee-deep snow. He found a good track entering a thick patch of spruce trees that had grown back as thick as dog hair thanks to a forest fire that had burned off that side of the mountains years before. It was so thick that I couldn't see the horse in front of me, much less a moose. Limbs were slapping me in the face as Luci and I squeezed through timber so thick we could barely fit between the trees. Suddenly my left boot hung firmly in the skeletal snag of a dead spruce. "Whoa!" I yelled, hauling back on the reins.

Luci kept right on walking.

"Whoa!" I screamed again with both hands now clasped around the saddle horn, which by then was my only point of contact with the saddle. Luci plodded on, and I was stretched like a rubber band between tree and saddle horn. Just as I was about to lose my grip, my boot came loose, catapulting me forward over Luci's right shoulder in a full gainer before landing in the posture of a dying cockroach in knee-deep snow. Thirty minutes later, Darren and Scott noticed that Luci was flying solo, so they stopped and waited for me to catch up. A nice gesture, I thought.

When I finally limped into sight, I was greeted with thunderous laughter and applause. Luci smiled politely.

After the festivities, everyone saddled up for the next great adventure. As I set my left foot in the stirrup and started to swing my right leg over the saddle, Luci bolted forward. The saddle cinch, loosened by my previous exercise, allowed the saddle to swing down under her belly and dump me face first into the snow, which became standard practice throughout the hunt.

More thunderous laughter and applause followed every time.

I am convinced that after that episode Luci knew she had the upper hand. Every time I attempted to mount the saddle, she'd wait until my right leg left the ground, and then she'd run forward, leaving me on my back, screaming obscenities at no one in particular.

Day after day we played her cute little game, but I finally got wise. I'd plant my left boot in the stirrup and then put some pressure on that stirrup as if I were going to throw my right leg over the saddle. But instead of following through with my right leg, as soon as she'd bolt, I'd jump back on the ground with both feet and haul back on the reins until she stopped.

This did complicate the game, though, because Luci knew that at some point I would have to actually go for it, and when I did, she'd be ready. This game we played kept my mind off the fact that moose were nowhere to be found. Darren toughed it out to the bitter end, but the moose prevailed. He did, however, shoot a beautiful caribou, which certainly helped justify 10 days of bronco riding.

At the end of the hunt we walked the horses down an extremely steep grade. When the trail flattened out, Scott told us it was alright to saddle up once more. Upon remounting, Luci did her bolt-and-run trick, but I was ready. I jumped back to the ground, hauled back on the reins and threatened Luci with her life. She reared up and came down on my right foot, pinning me to the ground.

The flesh took over at that point. The ensuing fisticuff ended in a draw between man and beast. "How much do you want for this stinkin' horse?" I screamed at the wrangler.

"The boss said he'd need about $700," he answered. Obviously, he'd heard that question before.

"Will you take MasterCard? I want to shoot this critter right here and now!"

"Naw, I'd need cash," he mumbled.

And that, dear reader, is the reason – the only reason – Luci is still plodding the mountain trails of the Yukon. To reiterate my perspective of mountain horses, the hunter should be offered the option of shooting his steed at the end of each hunt. That way the outfitter wouldn't have to worry about feeding horses through the winter, and the hunter would get to shoot the animal he wants to kill the most!

CHAPTER 22

Tongues of Fire

SOME OF THE FUNNIEST OF funnies actually happen in churches, proving beyond a shadow of a doubt that God has a wild sense of humor. A case in point happened in a church in Wyoming, which I shall not name so as not to embarrass a couple of fine "men of the cloth." Let's call them Brother Allen and Brother Benson.

Brother Allen is the pastor, originally from Texas. While you can't tear him away from Wyoming, there's still a good bit of Texas left in his heart – and in his stomach, especially when it comes to Mexican food. Jalapenos, habaneros and other fire-breathing peppers get to be addictive. As far as Brother Allen is concerned, the hotter the better. Happily, he found a little Mexican restaurant named Caliente's in the Wyoming town where he lives, and he's a regular customer, especially for breakfast.

Segue now to the Sunday morning when Brother Benson was the guest preacher at Brother Allen's church. On Sunday morning, Brother Allen suggested that they go out for breakfast before the morning service. Brother Benson was game, so off they went – straight to Caliente's.

Brother Allen ordered his regular plate of "los huevos mas caliente que de fuego de inferno." Brother Benson, having limited experience with Mexican breakfasts, decided to follow Brother Allen's lead rather than appear ignorant of such things. "Make that two," he said.

When the plates arrived, Brother Allen said grace and dove into his breakfast with the gusto of a starving bulldog. Brother Benson took a cautious bite and managed to choke down the hottest mouthful of food he had ever tasted. It took his breath away, but he managed to swallow the flaming eggs and habanero peppers. His face turned beet red. Beads of sweat formed on his forehead and began dripping like rain down onto his plate.

"Whaddaya think?" Brother Allen asked?

"Really nice," Brother Benson gagged as he inhaled his ice water, simultaneously mopping his brow with his napkin, wondering if his tongue and lips were going to blister.

Brother Allen was so consumed with his meal that he scarcely noticed that his guest was nibbling slowly on his flour tortillas and gulping ice water. Brother Benson silently prayed for a safe deliverance from "huevos caliente" and heaved a great sigh of relief when he and his host finally made their exit.

An hour later, after praise and worship, Brother Allen introduced Brother Benson to the congregation and invited him to the podium to preach. With burning lips, Brother Benson greeted everyone in the name of the Lord and then introduced the subject of his sermon: "The Empowering of the Holy Spirit."

For the first 15 minutes or so, he preached with clarity and authority, staying perfectly on point and commanding attention. He knew he was on a roll – perhaps even being carried by the very power about which he was preaching. He was explaining the significance of the tongues of fire on the Day of Pentecost when he felt an alien rumble in his bowels. After a momentary pause he continued, but a second and more determined rumble churned deep within him. It was then that Brother Benson began to stammer, realizing that the power of huevos caliente was upon him. He sputtered in pain as a wave of cramps rolled across his lower belly, nearly doubling him over and cutting short his breath. There was no graceful way to disguise his problem. Sweat popped out on his brow once more, and his face turned to deep crimson. He gritted his teeth, trying to hold back the inevitable. When he couldn't take it for one more second, he excused himself and, bent over at the waist, made a precarious dash for the men's room.

Brother Allen, sensing that something was very wrong, stepped up to the podium to fill the awkward air, quite unsure of what was to follow. At that moment Brother Benson had managed to hastily drop his drawers and back onto the toilet with fear and trepidation. As he squatted, all hell broke loose with the power of an incendiary bomb powered by untold volumes of compressed gas, all of which created an unrelenting cacophony of flutterblasts and moans the likes of which Brother Benson had never experienced. His inner war continued for another five minutes before he began to feel some degree of relief, to which he gasped, "Thank you Jesus."

Shortly thereafter he remembered that there was a sanctuary full of people that must be wondering what had happened to him. "Ohhhh noooooo," he moaned as he tried to think of how he would explain away his sudden disappearance, as one last blast of huevos caliente echoed off the men's room walls.

After gathering himself, he stood at the sink, washing his hands and splashing cold water on his face. He dried with a paper towel and looked at his blanched face in the mirror, desperately trying to remember exactly where he left off in his sermon.

"Oh yes," he whispered with relief, "tongues of fire."

With that he took a deep breath and left the men's room but was halted by the faint sounds of a roaring wind. This time it was not his own. Had God allowed the power of the spirit to fall on the congregation even in his absence? He could also hear what sounded like shrieks and howls, which, while not the norm, could possibly be the sounds of people responding to the Spirit. Suddenly Brother Benson was excited. Was this what he'd been praying for all these years?

He hurried down the corridor to the door to the sanctuary, and when he opened it the sounds that had been distant and muffled were now at full volume. He was shocked. The room appeared chaotic with some people doubled over, some prostrate on the floor, and some on their knees. Others were crying inconsolably and even wailing. But still others were cackling. Brother Benson wondered if Satan himself had overcome the congregation in his absence.

Brother Allen appeared before him with tears streaming down his face. "What's happening?" he stammered as Brother Allen gripped his arm and led him back into the corridor.

Brother Benson looked into Brother Allen's tear-stained face and anxiously asked, "Are you alright, Brother? What in heaven's name happened?"

Brother Allen stood there shaking for a moment, mopping his eyes with his handkerchief. Then he embraced Brother Benson and whispered into his ear: "Brother Benson," he sobbed, "you forgot to turn off your lapel mic."

CHAPTER 23

The Frozen Frilly Dilemma

IT WAS 35 BELOW ZERO at daybreak on that mid November morning in eastern Alberta in 1975. I was bundled up in my warmest hunting clothes and working my way slowly along a timbered fence line bordering some excellent pastureland where I knew that white-tailed bucks would be chasing does. My plan was to sneak quietly along in the knee-deep snow until I found a perfect vantage point beneath a tree where I could command a view of the surrounding area. November had been unusually warm and the deer hunting had been quite slow. This cold snap was just what was needed to kick the rut in to high gear, and I was going to be right in the middle of it.

I was carrying a Ruger No. 1B single shot rifle chambered for my favorite caliber: the Remington .25-06. It was a great shooter and if I ever felt confident of success it was on that morning. Even the sting of the bitter cold against my face didn't dampen my spirits.

I had married a Canadian lass a few years earlier and we had settled in Edmonton, Alberta, which was quite a departure for a native Texan who had never hunted in snow in his life before coming to Canada. One had to carefully prepare for this kind of cold or it could spell disaster. Thirty-five below zero has to be taken seriously. I'd say only the dedicated, hard-core hunters would venture out on a morning like that one, and I had not seen a living soul – neither man nor beast. Oh, there might have been a truck hunter patrolling around in the warmth of his pickup, but you weren't likely to see anybody else hunting on foot in that kind of weather.

The previous November I had taken my first Alberta whitetail: a 10-point scoring about 150 inches, but it was his body size that astounded me. I got 158 pounds of packaged meat back from the butcher! Being from Texas, I had always believed that Texas had the big deer, but I quickly learned that everything, especially white-tailed bucks, was not necessarily bigger and better in the Lone Star state. Now that I was properly educated about what constituted a "BIG" buck, I was anxious to bag one better than last year's.

I stepped cautiously along the fence line, trying to be as quiet as I could, but the dry snow squealed under my boots. I needed to quicken my pace to the observation point. As I hurried my steps, I hooked the toe of my right boot under a root buried in the snow. Before I could think, I tumbled face-first into a blistering cold snowdrift. I jumped up and began dusting the snow off my clothing, and I realized that my rifle had fallen muzzle-down. The barrel was plugged with snow.

I could not shoot the rifle unless I removed all the snow from the inside of the barrel, so I dropped the falling block action and ejected the cartridge. Next I broke off a small twig and began poking into the muzzle, but all I accomplished was to push the packed snow deeper down the barrel. I just knew that while I stood there completely helpless, the biggest buck in Alberta was going to bust out of the timber, and there would be nothing I could do.

Then it hit me: I could try to suck the snow out of the barrel. It would be safe enough because there was no doubt about the single shot being empty. "Brilliant," I thought as I lifted the muzzle to my lips. I sucked as hard as I could and, sure enough, I felt the plug of hardened snow pop into my mouth.

"Thornberry, you're a genius," I thought as I tried to remove the muzzle from my stinging lips. Then the horror of reality hit me. I, the aforementioned "genius," had just committed the Cardinal Canadian Winter No-No!

You don't touch metal with your lips in 35 below zero!

How in heaven's name was I going to warm up the muzzle of that rifle barrel and release my lips from its frozen grip?

I made a quick 360-degree survey to be sure no one was watching me. I felt like I just might be on Candid Camera. I envisioned the world record buck coming out of the timber and prancing around in front of me, knowing full well that I was harmless. In my vivid imagination I could hear him snickering! This was definitely not how I had planned my day!

The muzzle and I were in a very awkward jam that wasn't going to fix itself. I had two choices: 1) go back to camp with the muzzle still frozen to my lips and risk unbearable ridicule; or 2) just yank the barrel free myself. It didn't take long to decide on plan 2. Gritting my teeth, I gave a hard yank and the barrel came free. My lips stung like they were on fire and blood began trickling down my chin. Even this was not going to be easy to explain to my hunting partners. Then I looked down at the barrel of my rifle and there, wrapped around the muzzle, were my lips, frozen in place like some sadistic frilly decoration.

Things had instantly gone from bad to worse and suddenly my passion for the morning hunt dwindled into self-pity and self-consciousness. And there was that matter of burning, stinging lips, or at least the remainders thereof, and the freezing stream of blood dripping from my chin. It was a dismal finale.

It was years before I confessed my great mishap to anyone, but to my amazement every Canadian seems to have his or her own story of a tongue frozen to something. In their defense, most of their experiences happened to them when they were young, but still they knew better going in.

One girl had her tongue frozen to the outside of a school door handle. When the kid on the inside pulled the door open, he relieved her of the tip of her tongue. Another put the tip of her tongue against the steel rim of a large wagon wheel on a bitter winter day. Sure enough, it froze there. As a kid in Texas, I put the tip of my tongue against a frozen ice tray and got stuck. Odd that I didn't think of that when I wrapped my lips around the muzzle of the barrel of my Ruger No 1B. However, my grasp of the obvious has served me well since then. I am proud to announce that I have not frozen my tongue or my lips to anything since that fateful day!

CHAPTER 24

Fool's Gold

A FREAK EARLY SEPTEMBER BLIZZARD in 1972 would have been my last great adventure, were it not for a chance meeting with Marion Diesel northwest of Wandering River, Alberta. I was quickly mesmerized by his vast knowledge of wilderness living.

I won't recount all the details of that meeting because I covered it thoroughly in a previous book entitled "Trophies of the Heart" (chapter 1, A Moose for the Tenderfoot). Marion Diesel, then 65 years of age, became my mentor in the wild. He taught me to call moose and to trap beavers, lynx, fox and coyotes, and I spent every minute I could with him on his trap line, eager to learn anything he was willing to teach me. I was new to the North – a dry sponge trying to soak up all I had missed in my first 29 years of life. Marion and I became great friends. He was the gentle teacher and I was his student, anxious not only to learn about his present but also his past.

He and his family had come to Alberta from Oklahoma in a boxcar in 1905 when Marion was boy. He grew up in the hinterland, trapping and hunting and eventually working for the Alberta Forestry Department. But this story is rooted in Marion's adventurous life during the 1930s when he lived in the Northwest Territories. He was captain on a paddlewheel steamer on the mighty north-flowing Mackenzie River. He was also a prospector. Marion and his brother walked 700 miles one summer to stake claims in the wilderness.

They also once crossed the frozen Great Bear Lake in the dead of winter with a dogsled team. One day they were trapped in a blizzard, which created a virtual whiteout. They could not navigate by sight, so Marion used a map and compass to locate a small island that offered them some cover.

When they resumed their travel, the ice heaves were so tall on the lake that the dogs couldn't climb them. (Southern folks might not understand just what an ice heave is so I'll explain. After a lake freezes in the early winter, the ice expands, pushing against itself until it forms a crack that could be a mile long. Then the ice pushes upward along the broken seam, creating a sharp hill of ice that follows the contour of the crack. When the ice first heaves itself upward, there is open water below it but another ice layer soon forms on the water, creating a long hollow cavern of ice).

Imagine an ice heave so high that dogs couldn't climb it and you start to realize what Marion and his brother were up against. Ever practical when dealing with Mother Nature's curve balls, Marion used his axe to chop a hole into one side of the ice heave and out the other, large enough for he and his dogs to pass through. All in a day's work.

A year or so after Marion and I met, he told me a story about prospecting in the Northwest Territories that he said he had never told another soul. I was honored to hear it. As the story went, he cut trees along the creeks and rivers that flowed in the Mackenzie River. Then he would raft up the timber and float it north to Fort Norman, where he sold it to the Royal Canadian Mounted Police for their winter wood supply. While searching along the tributaries for timber, Marion was always mindful of mineral deposits that might warrant staking a claim. He encountered an unusual rock formation sticking up out of the trickle of a shallow creek, which, out of respect for Marion, I have chosen not to identify. Marion said the rock was rectangular – about the size of the top of an average coffee table, but much thicker. One end was submerged and the other a few inches above waterline.

This rock was unlike any he had seen before. He nonchalantly walked over to the outcropping and hit one corner with the flat back end of his axe, expecting to chip off a piece. To his amazement, the rock didn't chip – it bent! It most likely had a very high content of gold. To get a sample, he actually had to chop off a corner. He put the piece of rock in his pocket, noting its exact location, and then continued down the creek, cutting timber as he went.

"So, how much gold was in the rock?" I asked excitedly.

Marion explained that he decided against having the sample assayed while he was in the far north because it was impossible to keep a secret and he, with good reason, was concerned about getting killed by unscrupulous claim jumpers and robbers. He brought the rock home with him to Alberta, always intending to go back for the mother lode. His subsequent assay proved his suspicions. It was loaded with gold.

Marion wasn't telling me this to garner interest in a return trip. It was just a part of his past. But this was about gold, possible wealth, and real adventure. I jumped on it like a chicken on a June bug and insisted that he and I go back to the Northwest Territories to find the gold. He wasn't opposed to the idea, but he wasn't sure how we'd finance such a trip.

I knew a number of well-heeled businessmen in Edmonton and made them a profit-sharing offer in return for financing the trip. In those days – the early 70s – the Canadian government offered big tax write-offs for mining exploration so the investors had little to lose and a lot to gain. So, in July of

1973, Marion and I flew from Edmonton to Norman Wells, Northwest Territories, to search for gold.

The first thing I realized was that the "real" north was much bigger, more remote and a great deal wilder than I had expected. We had planned our exploration the old fashioned way, carrying everything we would need on our backs. That included a small two-man tent, clothes, freeze dried food, tin plates and utensils, axes, rock hammers, etc. The following day we loaded up a single engine Beaver on floats, heading south toward Fort Norman. From there we headed southeast into the Franklin Mountain range, which was dotted with hundreds if not thousands of small lakes. It was dawning on me that I had bitten off more than I had ever attempted to chew. It was a little frightening to get dropped off in the middle of nowhere, but the company of a man that had done this all his life comforted me. Marion had an inner compass that always took us where we wanted to go. I trusted that this trip would be no different.

When the plane tipped its nose toward one of a thousand nameless lakes, I wondered how the pilot could ever tell one from another. How would he know this particular lake a month later? When the pontoons slid up against the shore, Marion and I jumped out, unloaded our gear, and reaffirmed our return date with the pilot. Then he flew into dark gray clouds. As the drone of the engine faded, the silence of the mountains screamed in my ears. There was nothing to hear

–just the void of a silent wilderness that didn't even acknowledge our presence.

Since the lake where we landed had no identifiable name on the map, we christened it "Little Thornberry Lake." We quickly went about pitching our tent and roughing out a campsite while the rain started falling. Soon we were forced inside for shelter from a thunderstorm with winds so strong that we thought our tent might be ripped from the ground. Lightning cracked and flashed around us, and the ground quaked in response. This was not the kind of welcome I was expecting from Mother Nature, but Marion seemed to take it all in stride. I tried to cover my concerns with false bravado. I was faking it pretty well until lightning struck a dead spruce tree only 40 yards from the tent. We could see the lightning bolt through the canvas. The spruce exploded into a billion flaming cinders that filled the sky as magnificently as any 4th of July fireworks display. A number of the burning cinders rained down on the roof of our tent, burning little holes through it, which let in the raindrops. So much for creature comforts.

That night I got a crash course in the woes of holes in small tents. The mosquitoes and black flies poured in and chewed us into oblivion. There was no escape. Our repellent seemed to attract them. At times I thought I might lose my mind. I had never experienced anything like it, and just knowing I was helpless forced me into a constant state of fighting panic.

Marion had dealt with these clouds of man-eaters before, and he had one short-term solution that offered us relief, albeit brief. He would pile up the white, dried caribou moss and set it on fire. When it burned there was hardly any flame, but it created a plume of thick, white smoke. The bugs didn't like it. We would take a deep breath and hold it while we stuck our heads into the white smoke. The relief lasted only as long as one could hold his breath, but it was worth every second away from the black flies. The problem with black flies is that you don't feel their bite when you're being bitten. But within a few minutes afterward the bite begins to burn and itch. By the time I'd been at Little Thornberry Lake 12 hours, I was a walking, festering sore.

Marion had picked this lake for our base camp because it was close to the headwaters of the creek where he had found the gold. Our plan was to leave most of our base camp behind and travel as light as possible to the headwaters. Our topographical map indicated that Little Thornberry Lake was approximately eight miles from the headwaters as the crow flies. But we weren't crows and we weren't flying.

We took a compass bearing and found that we had to take a northeast heading. That sounded simple enough, but I soon learned that nothing in the Franklin Mountains was going to be simple. We found no trails of any kind, much less trails heading northeast, so we essentially had to bulldoze our bodies through head-high alders that wrapped around our ankles and ground us to a halt every few feet. Being bound up in alders offered the black flies carte blanche. We were sitting ducks. I chopped at the trees, trying to free myself, but the alders only bounded away. Likewise they were impossible to break with our hands. It was a hellish eight miles, probably closer to 12 given all the circumnavigation required.

Late in the day we found the headwaters of what I shall refer to as Fool's Gold Creek. It was just a trickle when we found it, which was in keeping with our plan to make the trip in July, when the water would be at its lowest. Low water was essential for our search of the creek bottom. We planned to follow the full length of the creek all the way to the Mackenzie River so that we would miss nothing. We would have to return to base camp and bring the rest of our equipment to the headwaters and then follow the creek slowly downstream, taking our time to explore every nook and cranny.

It was satisfying to stand at the little trickle of the headwaters, even though the trip to locate it was hellish. I got a glimpse of what true explorers must have felt when they made their discoveries. I also had a renewed appreciation for Lewis and Clark who endured the cruel whip of Mother Nature for years as they pushed bravely to the Pacific Ocean. Twelve miles through alder-choked boulders was about as much adventure as I could handle for one day.

As I stood on the banks of the creek, I saw something dimple the surface of the water. Being a fly fisherman I knew a fish had sucked in some kind of insect. Instantly I moved into fish mode. (Knowing that there is a fish present and not attempting to catch it is unthinkable.) This was a special challenge since the only fishing tackle I had was back at base camp. I tied a 15-inch piece of string to the tip of a limber willow branch. Then I tied a small safety pin enhanced with a small raveling of red wool yarn I had pulled from the top of my socks to the other end of the string. The first time I flipped the awkward offering onto the water, I was obliged by a 15-inch Arctic grayling that grabbed the yarn like it was his favorite dish. Hauling back on the willow branch, I cart wheeled him over my shoulder onto the bank behind me, where the safety pin fell out of his mouth. I pounced on him like a hungry cat and announced that he would soon be a part of a special wilderness fish dinner. The grayling, having never seen a human, much less red sock yarn, continued to oblige. Marion enjoyed a grayling dinner there on the creek bank before heading back to base camp.

I experienced a sense of survivor satisfaction during that meal and silently patted myself on the back for a little wilderness ingenuity. After all, I had provided food, stupid food admittedly, but food nonetheless.

On our trek back to base camp it began to rain lightly, which made the alders and boulders as slippery as they were obnoxious. We were soaked to the bone by the time were arrived back at Little Thornberry Lake – just in time to crawl into a leaking tent and a couple of wet sleeping bags. It was miserable to be sure, but on a positive note, a wet sleeping bag protected us from the wrath of the black flies, which now lined the ridge of our little tent by the millions. This was clearly going to be a mind over matter endeavor on a level I had never known.

Time was hard for the mind to measure since the sun shone 24 hours a day. Oddly, the birds seemed to know the difference between night and day because about the time one would expect darkness to fall, they would go to roost. Nature provided them with an internal clock – one that I was obviously missing. I quickly lost all track of time. With no darkness, life seemed surreal. The constant light eventually began to feel like a punishment. Without night – dark night – days seemed rather meaningless. I'm sure the reverse would also be true in the winter months in that land when darkness consumed the clock.

During the night the rain intensified into a real downpour, and the sky was slate gray across the horizon. We decided to wait until it stopped before we hauled all our gear to the creek. After 24 hours the rain subsided. We packed everything into our backpacks and headed once more through the soggy alders and slippery boulders, stopping periodically to make a smudge fire of caribou moss to fight the flies. Our trip was a silent for the most part, save for an occasional slapping of the black flies or cursing of the alder tangles. We hiked hour after hour in the rain, glancing up occasionally to see if there was any break in the clouds. There wasn't.

Marion and I were like drowned rats when we finally stepped onto the banks of Fool's Gold Creek. We were exhausted and miserable, but our physical inconveniences paled by the emotions we experienced when we realized that the creek was swelling with rainwater.

The water was five feet deep where it had been 18 inches two days before and it was rapidly rising. Water was our worst enemy in this endeavor. Without low water, all was for naught. The creek continued to swell to a depth of 12 feet in a matter of hours. It would be days before the water level dropped enough for us to search the creek bottom. We decided to pack back to Little Thornberry Lake and wait it out. And wait it out we did.

For dreary days on end, the sky remained slate gray and the rain fell, intent upon washing us off the face of the Earth. Keeping a fire going was essential. If it died it would be a real test to light another with nothing but soggy wood. In a matter of days, we had burned all the dead wood within reasonable walking distance from our camp. Next we cut small green spruce and balsam trees. The green trees burned quickly but their sap produced a very hot fire, burning like kerosene.

Marion and I spent the days foraging for trees of a manageable size to carry back to the fire. In so doing we got soaked to the bone. Once the new trees were flaming we would warm up and actually start to dry out, but when the fire began to die, it was back into the timber.

Our tent shrank and was subsequently not long enough for my 6'2" frame. Marion, at 5'6", still fit. Even though we had patched the myriad holes burnt into the roof by the flaming embers of our first night, we found that the condensation created by two bodies in the tent created as much water as the rain created on the outside. That was the pre-Gortex era, before there was an intelligent way to control condensation. We did our best, but I can't say that our efforts were necessarily intelligent. Perhaps "desperation" is a better description.

Since sleeping in the tent with Marion was no longer an option, I employed my very best Boy Scout talents and built myself a shelter of spruce boughs and garbage bags. It was an ugly addition to the landscape but still a shelter. There I learned that a soaked sleeping bag by any other name is still a hellish way to try to sleep. When you try to roll over and squish water from one part of the bag to another it tends to make you homesick. And homesick I was. Mother Nature's whipping was starting to tell on me. It was the first time in my life I was ever trapped in a condition that I could not leave or make better. It worked on my mind. I was becoming sullen and moody. Marion could see it, too.

One night, after a long day of cutting green trees to keep the fire going, I pulled the cold, wet sleeping bag up around my ears and tried to imagine my way out of this reality. It didn't work. Thought I couldn't alter the misery, I found some strange comfort in hating it. But being miserable and trying to hate it enough to change it is pure folly. I was getting in a bad way.

I don't know what time it was – maybe 11 p.m. or midnight. It wasn't dark of course but the sky was still slate gray and the rain continued. I heard Marion say "goodnight" from the tent. I didn't answer but I remember thinking that there was nothing good about that night. Within a minute or so, I heard Marion's harmonica. He was playing "There's No Place Like Home."

The irony broke my depression and I actually laughed out loud. Marion was suffering too, but he was mentally tougher than I was. It was then that I realized what "mind over matter" really meant, and that little song playing on a harmonica became an anthem. I was going to get as tough as the weather, one way or another!

After days of rain at Little Thornberry Lake, Marion decided that we had nothing to lose by seeing some new country, so we packed up our soggy gear and headed into the mountains just to look around. The first thing we noticed was that there wasn't a flat spot large enough to pitch a tent anywhere.

Everything was up and down – never flat. One afternoon we found some mysterious animal tracks that could only have been made by mountain sheep. They were the size of large deer tracks but with rounded sheep-like hooves. There were many such tracks the same size, so that ruled out caribou. The only problem was that there were not supposed to be any mountains east of the Mackenzie River. But if the tracks weren't made by deer, moose or caribou, that only left sheep.

We pitched our tent in a small bowl-shaped swale where we were sure not to slide off the mountainside. I curled up to fit the shortened version of our shrunken tent. We pulled our wet sleeping bags up around our ears and went to sleep. I kept my little Winchester lever action .30-30 between us in case of an emergency. In the wee hours, I was awakened by the sounds of something woofing, growling and slapping the tent. At first I thought I was dreaming, but when I opened my eyes I was astounded to see Marion sitting up with his sleeping bag fallen to his waist while he flailed the tent wall with his fists. On the other side of the thin canvas was a very upset animal.

I reached for the .30-30 in panic, but before I could figure out what to do with it the commotion stopped. Marion explained that while he was asleep, an animal, presumably a black bear, put his front paws upon the tent roof and it collapsed with both front feet and a layer of canvas on Marion's face. Marion came up slugging. The surprised critter snapped back but finally left us alone. The ground was so hard and rocky that we could find no tracks to positively identify the intruder. (Perhaps we were the intruders.) In any case it was one exciting way to wake up from a sound sleep. Marion was fine, but I was shaken.

I crawled out and put on some of my driest soggy clothes. Marion crawled out behind me and tried to stand up but couldn't get his balance. He stumbled around and finally had to sit back down. As bad as things were, I was suddenly overtaken by a new fear. What if Marion was sick and needed help? What if he died out there? That would leave only me, and that idea terrified me. After all, I was a greenhorn on a wilderness adventure, out of my depth. It was a humbling, if not a terrifying experience, but eventually Marion's equilibrium returned and he was fine. I cannot describe my relief.

After a couple of days climbing around in the mountains we returned to Little Thornberry Lake and set up our camp as before. That evening I decided it was high time for a bath and although the lake water was frigid, I could stand myself no longer. I stripped naked, grabbed some soap, and plunged into the lake up to my eyes to protect as much of myself as I could from the black flies, which were so enchanted by the "other white meat."

After adjusting to the water temperature, I was having a very enjoyable bath. I had my back to the bank, giving myself one last rinse, when the water exploded behind me. I spun around just in time to see a cow and calf moose charging into the lake with me. For a tense moment, we stared at each other, unsure of what would happen next.

To say I felt vulnerable would be a gross understatement. Standing naked, chest deep in water, armed with only a bar of soap makes for a relatively poor defense against pretty well anything.

The moose and I were less than 10 yards apart. I held my breath for a minute, and the cow and calf casually waded down the shoreline, eating vegetation growing along the lakeshore. They seemed happy, so I was happy. I waded out of the lake, dried off, put on my clothes and watched them feed. I admit that I soon started seeing the moose in a totally different light. After all, we had been eating a steady diet of freeze dried food that was so bad it made me long for a good bowl of sawdust. Now my eyes beheld hundreds of pounds of prime moose steaks within easy rifle range. I could almost taste the back straps frying, but the weather was so warm that raw meat would spoil in hours – certainly in less time than it would take to eat even a small moose. I'm sure it wasn't moose season anyway, but there wasn't any law against dreaming of a good moose steak. The pair frequented the shores of Little Thornberry Lake every evening. Eventually they became like family.

Blueberries growing in abundance offered respite from freeze dried food. We had taken some Bisquick with us so that we could make bannock now and then, or skillet biscuits, which turned out to be delicacies in our wilderness diet.

One afternoon I was picking blueberries on a hillside, down on all fours with a little pail, thinking about the skillet pie I was going to cook that evening. When I glanced up there was a black bear in the same berry patch not 20 feet in front of me. As with the moose, we spent a couple of moments staring each other down. Eventually the bear began to eat blueberries as he faced me. He acted very nonchalant about it, but he was watching me at all times. I remained frozen so as not to disturb the peace, which I felt was of ultimate importance. Unarmed and in such close proximity to the bear, I was still fascinated by the way he would delicately pick a single berry from the bush with his lips. He was a most polite bear with enviable table manners. He ventured off to another berry patch after awhile, and I continued filling my bucket for the evening pie.

The rain kept us in a holding pattern at Little Thornberry Lake. There would be no returning to the headwaters of the creek, so we tried to occupy ourselves with whatever we could find to break the boredom and take our minds off the miserable weather. One day I asked Marion what he thought we might find on the other side of the lake. I suppose it was a stupid question. We would obviously find more empty wilderness and more rain, but at least it would offer us something to do, so we decided to go for it. It didn't take us long to realize that we couldn't navigate around either end of the lake. There was a muskeg at both ends – an impossible quagmire just waiting to swallow the fool that stepped in it. The only way across the lake was to make a raft.

Well, Huckleberry Finn at your service! I had never built a raft, but I was anxious to give it a go. The problem was that there were no big trees anywhere near our camp. A few big logs would have been perfect, but since there were none we would have to use many little logs about the diameter of baseball bats. When we rafted up enough small timber to float two men, the craft was a virtual cube of tiny tree trunks, most of which was underwater once Marion and I boarded. We nailed tin camp plates on the ends of limbs to use as paddles. As hard as we could paddle, we could barely detect movement. We were about to call the venture off as a bad idea when the wind came up and started blowing us into the lake. The good news was that we were heading in the right direction. The bad news was that we'd have to paddle back against the wind. There was nothing we could do but go along for the ride.

As Marion was making a stroke with his paddle, I saw a yellow flash in the water like a bolt of lightning that hit the tin plate and ricocheted into the deep. It was a big fish looking for a big meal. Any fish that would strike a tin plate in the water had my undivided interest.

"Jackfish ... a big jackfish," Marion declared.

Jackfish is a Canadian term for Northern Pike. They are aggressive feeders and, in such wilderness environs, as dumb as fence posts. I had a 5-inch long Len Thompson brass spoon and 50 yards of green ice fishing cord in my daypack, though I have no idea what I might use it for. Suddenly I had a plan. I tied the lure to the green cord, twirled it above my head like a lariat and threw it as far as I could, then quickly retrieved it hand-over-hand. On the first throw a pike nearly tore the cord out of my hands, but eventually I got things under control and dragged a 20-pounder onto our makeshift raft. It was simply amazing. I couldn't have been using a more primitive approach, and I couldn't have caught more fish with a stick of dynamite! I continued to catch pike at will until we neared the opposite shore, at which time it was all hands on deck to make sure our cube of sticks didn't get high-centered on a sharp rock. In such case two mortal men would have been helpless.

After bottoming on sand, we tied our vessel to a tree and set off to explore this new territory. It was amazingly similar to what we had just left, but at least it was NEW country. After an afternoon of climbing up rock spires and poking around among suspicious looking rocks, the net discovery for our efforts was an ancient prospector's hammer and one weathered boot sole. We were not the first adventurous souls to set foot there. One's imagination can run wild with any number of scenarios surrounding the hammer and boot sole, but I was sure that if the relics could have spoken they would have said, "Get the hell out of here and never come back."

While just speculation, it did summarize my sentiments about the whole of the experience to date. How ironic: we had come for the hidden treasure that promised us the good life. But somehow we didn't notice the wink that accompanied the promise. We waited until the wind died and started the voyage back across Little Thornberry Lake. Several million strokes of our tinplate paddles later, we arrived right back where we started. It was Groundhog Day – no doubt.

When the sky is perpetually slate gray, the mind will play tricks on itself. The want for a trace of blue becomes so great that you actually think you see it, thought it's not really there. The power of anxiety, I guess. Time after time I could have sworn I saw blue sky, but it wasn't really there. We eventually came to grips with the fact that there would be no hope of looking for the gold, so we were hunkered down in the rain just trying to maintain our sanity until the plane returned to deliver us from the nightmare.

One morning as we squatted by our blazing fire of greenwood, an amazing thing happened – the rain turned to snow. Great white flakes drifted lazily and the temperature dropped significantly. We were initially stunned, not so much by the snow, but because something was different in our world. It lifted our spirits. I remember it as if it were yesterday. When Marion looked up and saw snow falling, he snatched up his tin camp plate and a spoon and began banging on the plate, singing, and dancing around the campfire. It was wonderful – like Christmas. I joined him and we whooped and hollered like little kids celebrating our good fortune. The snow would not make our lives any easier, but it was something other than rain. I can recall but few occasions that have brought me such unbridled exuberance.

The snow brought new concerns. We had not planned for winter weather in July. We had long given up on being dry, but now staying warm was not an option. It was essential. This meant that the fire could never go out. It meant slugging through the snow-clad dog-hair spruce timber in order to find a tree big enough to cut and fuel the fire. Subsequently, shift work was implemented. When one man needed to sleep, the other would keep the fire going. Oddly, this survival mode added new purpose to our lives because we had something important to do – stay alive. As a bonus, the plummeting temperature locked down the black flies and mosquitoes. That was another reason to rejoice.

When the day finally arrived for the floatplane to return, we watched the sky solemnly. We were socked in and we knew it.

The plane would have to fly dangerously low through thick cloud cover before getting low enough to see the lake. Since bush pilots necessarily fly by sight, we knew it was unlikely that the plane would be able to land, if it came at all. So, we were not really surprised when we heard the drone of the single engine above the clouds. It reminded me of someone lost at sea who could see the search party but could not be seen. My heart sunk to a new low as the droning faded and the plane returned to its base without us.

The following morning the plane returned again with the same results, then again in the afternoon, but we fared no better. But the next morning for the first time since the rain had started, we actually saw real blue sky. The plane flew over us, but we could see it! It made a loop, nosed into the wind and touched down for the second time on Little Thornberry Lake. The sight of that plane taxiing toward us was an unspeakable event. I had encountered more adversity than I knew existed on this trip, and I was humbly satisfied that I had survived.

Again I marveled at the sight of Little Thornberry Lake passing beneath the wing. It still seemed like one little wet dot amidst a million just like it. I recalled my initial doubts about the pilot ever finding that lake again, and I offered a deep prayer of thanks that he did.

Back in Norman Wells, Marion and I rented a room in a motel that was essentially a giant mobile home. It was funny – a motel with wheels. We each had a long awaited hot shower, put on clean, dry clothes, went to the restaurant and ordered cheeseburgers and tall glasses of cold milk. It tasted divine after a prolonged diet of freeze dried food (if you could call it that).

However, the motel room seemed stuffy and smelled like stale grease. It made me uncomfortable, and I actually missed the fresh cold air I had become used to breathing. Similarly, as I tossed and turned and tried to sleep that night, I felt a bit claustrophobic. The room was too warm. It made me sweat. I missed the clean smell of spruce trees in the rain.

Made in the USA
Lexington, KY
30 December 2018